Ladakh
Individuality Vs State

Attention Authors

'We Convert Fighters into Writers'. That's the motto of Manas Publications for more than four decades. Our message to the world is that India can win the battle not only by the bullet but also by the pen. There is no dearth of intellectuals in our country, but their knowledge is confined to them only. No sincere effort has been made by any other publisher to channelise their knowledge in national interest. That is why the talent of a large number of intellectuals remains latent. An author transforms his knowledge into a manuscript, and it is our job to spread his/her knowledge by converting it into a beautiful book. For over four decades, Manas has been motivating the intellectuals by publishing their manuscripts and would like to publish your manuscript too. If you or your colleagues have any manuscript ready for publication or are working on it, kindly contact us with detailed synopsis and list of contents. We will transform your work into a valuable publication. If you wish, we can also suggest you the suitable subjects for writing the books related to your area of expertise. Manas is known for its publishing quality and commitments. We take utmost care in production and give wide publicity to the book as well as its author through our national and international distribution network.

Ladakh
Individuality Vs State

Harish K. Thakur
Department of Political Science
Govt College for Girls, RKMV, Shimla

Manas Publications
(We Convert Fighters into Writers)
New Delhi- 110002 (INDIA)

MANAS PUBLICATIONS
(Publishers for IAS, IPS, IFS, IRS, Defence, Press, Judges etc.)
(Publishers, Library Suppliers, Importers & Exporters)
4402/5-A, Ansari Road (Opp. HDFC Bank)
Darya Ganj, New Delhi-110 002 (India)
Off: ✆ 011-23260783, 23265523, Res: 011-23842660
Fax: 011-23272766
E-mail: manaspublications@gmail.com
manaspublications@yahoo.com
Website: www.manaspublications.in

2015
ISBN: 978-81-7049-478-2
Rs. 695/-

Designed at
Manas Publications

Printed in India at
RK Print Services, Delhi
and published by Mrs Suman Lata for
Manas Publications, 4402/5-A,
Ansari Road, (Opp HDFC Bank),
Darya Ganj, New Delhi-110 002 (INDIA)

CONTENTS

	Preface	7
1.	Introduction	9
2.	Ladakh: Land and the People	21
3.	Inter-Regional Divergence in Jammu & Kashmir: A Historical Perspective	47
4.	Inter-Regional Divergence and Ladakh–I	119
5.	Inter-Regional Divergence and Ladakh–II	159
6.	Concluding Remarks	203
	Bibliography	221
	Index	229

Preface

The task of a research pursuit especially when it undertakes a remote area like Ladakh is always full of anxiety, adventure and enrichment. The present book is the outcome of the project that was sanctioned by ICSSR (Indian Council of Social Science Research) in March 2010. The endeavour had its own implications since the horrid topography and inclement weather allow restricted movement in the region. The unpleasant incident of cloud burst at Leh and surrounding areas in the summer, a natural disaster so rare in the desert like land of Ladakh and the incessant rains made things difficult for the researcher. However, the ever cooperative people of Ladakh and unrelenting support of friends made the task much easier.

The book is devided into six chapters. The introductory chapter specifies the research problem, reviews literature and delineates the area of study. The second chapter elaborates the physiography, society, culture, economy, polity and administration of the region of Ladakh. Third chapter views the problem from historical perspective and presents an inter-regional comparison of socio-economic and cultural dimensions of the regions of Ladakh, Jammu and Kashmir. The fourth and fifth chapters largely probe the socio-economic, cultural, administrative and political factors that lie underneath the general discontent of Ladakhis and are causative of divergence among them. The last chapter presents the findings of the study and registers certain recommendations with the belief that they would be carried forward to the concerned authorities for consideration.

I would like to thank all those who have helped me a lot during my research. I would also like to express my gratitude to Advocate Nurboo Gialchan, currently MLC, Jammu and Kashmir State Legislative Assembly and P.T. Kunzang, General Secretary of LBA for the constant support they provided during the research. I also express my gratitude to Dr. Wangcchuk Dorje, Principal, Centre for Buddhist Studies Leh, Principal Government College Leh, Dr. Prem Singh Jina and Dr. Raj Kumar for necessary help as and when I required.

My sincere thanks to Prof. Naresh Mahajan, Principal, Government College for Girls (RKMV) Shimla, for his unwavering support in the execution of current research programme. Special thanks are due to Dr. Naresh Verma, Associate Professor, Department of Public Administration, G.C. Sanjauli, Shimla; Advocate Mohinder Pal Jaraik and Mr. D.S. Thakur who took special interest in this endeavour and helped me greatly in the execution of field survey and collection of data.

Harish K Thakur

Chapter 1

Introduction

Ladakh is one of the sparsely populated regions of India. It has strived for centuries against its hostile environ and the people. It is one of the highest inhabited places of the world that represents the vast splendours of nature on the one hand and threshold of border conflict between India and China on the other. Its strategic location and rich minerals make it a region of stupendous significance for the country. Very much like Jammu and Kashmir, the inclusion of the region in the state of Jammu and Kashmir is again a matter of historical debate and people of the region still look for better alternatives to safeguard their regional, cultural identity.

Over the decades Ladakhis have raised their demands for the protection of their unique cultural identity demanding either separate Statehood or Union Territory status. These demands are further accentuated by several factors like regional divergence within the state which manifests at geographical, social and cultural levels, dominance of valley at the administrative and political levels, militancy in Kashmir, sense of relative deprivation, under development and more significantly the fear of loss of their cultural identity. Within the region of Ladakh also there are sub-regional identities at times heading for minor stand offs.

Of late, fundamentalism and terrorism in the valley has catapulted the state of Jammu & Kashmir to the forefront at international level. Militancy which has claimed more than 30,000 lives since 1988 refuses to die down and a peaceful solution still seems to be elusive. The resultant of anti-Valley feelings in the two other regions of Ladakh and Jammu compounded by multiple factors has exerted a lot of pressure on the state and the Union governments. The problem of Kashmir is probably the most widely studied issue in India and abroad by the scholars, academicians, and journalists alike. Literature ranges from polemical assertions, sympathetic suggestions, analytical statements, and historical surveys to experimenting with the diverse political arrangements and theories that mostly adorn the bookshelves of the experts.

Most of the works study the external factors such as cross-border terrorism, the role of ISI, Jamaat-I-Islami, Lashkar-e-Taiyyiba etc. and the Muslim countries besides lamenting over the trail of events that followed the partition. However, very few of them take into account the most significant aspect of the problem, the inter-regional relations within the state of Jammu and Kashmir. The inter-regional diversity and tensions between the regions of Ladakh, Jammu and Kashmir probably bear more significant impact on the current sequence of events in the state than anything else.

The state of Jammu and Kashmir, the largest of the formerly princely states of India, is about the size of Great Britain and has an area of 2,22,236 sq. kms. It is situated in the extreme north between Latitude 32°.15' and 37°.5' north and Longitude 72°.35' and 80°.20' East. The physiography of Kashmir in relation to India is economically most important, in as much as the great reservoirs, from which is drawn the waters that nourish the vast plains of the lands of five rivers, are contained herein. Here are born infant streams which feed the Indus, the Jhelum, the Chenab, the Ravi and to a great extent the Sutlej also.[1]

The state of Jammu and Kashmir is a sensitive and strategically important area as it shares its borders with Tibet, in the North-East with the Sinkiang Province of China, to the North with Afghan territory of Wakhan, a few miles away with the territory of Turkmenistan and to the West with Pakistan. The Britishers used the territory of Kashmir both as a base for incursions into Tibet and Afghanistan and also as a buffer between these territories and British India.

A major demographic and geographic change in the state followed the ceasefire Agreement of January 1, 1949 which terminated the armed conflict between India and Pakistan. It left thousands of sq kms of area in the control of the latter. The area included Gilgit and Northern frontier dependencies of the state, Scardu in the district of Ladakh, Pothoari speaking Western tract comprising the district of Muzzafarabad in Kashmir Province along with a large part of the Poonch Jagir in Jammu Province. Mirpur district and its surrounding areas of Jammu Province were also lost to Pakistan.[2]

According to the census report of 2011,the total population of the state was 1,25,48,926 out of which Kashmir region (Anantnag, Pulwama, Srinagar, Badgam,

Baramulla, Kupwara , Kulgam, Bandipore, Ganderbal and Shupian districts) constituted 69,07,623 (55.04 percent). Jammu region (Jammu, Kathua, Punch, Rajauri, Udhampur, Reasi, Samba, Kishtwar, Ramban and Doda) contributes 53,50781 (42.63 percent) to the state population. The region of Ladakh (Kargil and Leh districts) contributed just about 2,90,492 (2.31 percent). For a comparative district wise population of the state (2001-2011) see Table No.1.1.

Table No 1.1

Ranking of Districts by Population Size, 2001 - 2011

Rank 2011	District	Population 2011	% age to state Popul-ation 2011	Population 2001	% age to state Popul-ation 2001	Rank 2001
1	2	3	4	5	6	7
1	Jammu	1526406	12.16	1357077	13.38	1
2	Srinagar	1269751	10.12	1027670	10.13	2
3	Anantnag	1070144	8.53	778408	7.67	4
4	Baramula	1015503	8.09	843892	8.32	3
5	Kupwara	875564	6.98	650393	6.41	5
6	Badgam	735753	5.86	607181	5.99	6
7	Rajouri	619266	4.93	483284	4.76	8
8	Kathua	615711	4.91	511455	5.04	7
9	Pulwama	570060	4.54	441275	4.35	10
10	Udhampur	555357	4.43	459486	4.53	9
11	Punch	476820	3.80	372613	3.67	12
12	Kulgam	422786	3.37	394026	3.88	11
13	Doda	409576	3.26	320256	3.16	13
14	Bandipore	385099	3.07	304886	3.01	14
15	Samba	318611	2.54	272539	2.69	15
16	Reasi	314714	2.51	247694	2.44	16
17	Ganderbal	297003	2.37	217907	2.15	17
18	Ramban	283313	2.26	214944	2.12	18

19	Shupiyan	265960	2.12	211332	2.08	19
20	Kishtwar	231037	1.84	190843	1.88	20
21	Leh	147104	1.17	117232	1.16	22
22	Kargil	143388	1.14	119307	1.18	21
	J&K	12548926	100.0	10143700	100.0	

Source: Census of India 2001 and 2011

Jammu & Kashmir is a state that broadly comprises of three regions –Muslim majority Kashmir, Hindu majority Jammu and Buddhist majority area of Ladakh. Ladakh region which is largest in area (about 70 percent of the state) is sparsely inhabited and accounts for only 2.31percent of the population. Kashmir, which has only about 11 percent of the area of the state, accounts for about 55.05 percent of the population. Against it Jammu region has 19 percent of the area with about 42.64 percent of the population.

Here one can notice from Table No 1.1 that the region of Kashmir has witnessed a rise of 1.15 percent population in the last decade when compared to the census report of 2001. Against it the region of Jammu has witnessed a fall in the population at about 1.04 percent. The region of Ladakh has also registered a slight decrease of 0.3 percent.[3]

The population composition of the three regions according to religion as shown in Table No. 1.2 makes them more distinct and diverse. Considering the geographical dissimilarities and the cultural variations the state exhibits a sheer contrast from the rest of the Indian states and if we club these attributes together no two regions are alike. In fact, the heterogeneity that they reflect is hardly seen in any other state of India.

Table No 1.2
Religion-wise Population of Jammu & Kashmir

Divisions	Population	Muslims %	Hindus %	Sikhs %	Buddhists %
Kashmir (53.9%)	5,476,970	97.16	1.84	0.88	0.11
Jammu (43.7%)	4,430,191	30.69	65.23	3.57	0.51
Ladakh (2.3%)	2,36,539	47.40	6.22	--	45.87
Jammu & Kashmir	10,143,700	66.97	29.63	2.03	1.36

Statistics compiled from Census of India, 2001: District Profiles

Since passing of the power to Kashmiris from Jammu based Dogras there has been a tug of war between these regions, each one advocating its interests in a different way. Kashmir which is ethnically more homogeneous on account of common race, language and religion stands for more autonomy whereas the regions of Jammu and Ladakh which are ethnically of different stocks have taken varied stances ranging from the status of separate Statehood or Union Territory to their merger with other states of India.

In this intra-regional battle for dominance the worst sufferer is the region of Ladakh. The reasons behind are not far to see. Being sparsely populated, the region of Ladakh is a backward region partially because of difficult terrain and rough passages and also because of sheer neglect by various state regimes. This discrimination has resulted in the form of demand for UT status raised by Ladakh Buddhist Association. The sense of relative deprivation among Ladakhis vis-à-vis Kashmir and Jammu has brewed a great deal of discontent among Ladakhis. Moreover, the Muslim majority area of Kargil within Ladakh, that has been overshadowed by jehadis of the valley provide a new dimension and add to the complexity of the problem.

In this endeavour we propose to study the relations of Ladakh vis-à-vis Jammu and Kashmir, which, no doubt has a direct bearing on the overall personality of the state. The intra-regional tensions within the state have to a great extent alienated the people of the valley. The process of economic development and political democratization in J&K in general and Ladakh in particular needs to be keenly studied. During the course of study the popular demands of LBA, LUTF and the special favours accorded to the people of Ladakh (tribal status and Ladakh Autonomous Hill Council) also requires minute study so that the crux of the problem could be delineated. This study might diffuse regional tensions within the state of J&K which in turn will have an obvious positive impact on the mindset of the valley based people.

Objectives of the Study

The prime objectives of the current study are to explore the following points and perspectives of the people of Ladakh region:

a. To delineate upon the demands of the people of Ladakh for more political autonomy vis-à-vis the people of Jammu and Kashmir.

b. To study the impact of militancy in the Valley on the people of Ladakh.

c. To understand and study the regional aspirations for a separate political status, share in power structure, and the feeling of relative deprivation among Ladakhis.

d. To analyze the influence of the process of globalization, study the patterns of development and the emerging trends in socio-economic, political and cultural life of Ladakhis.

e. The recommendation and utilization of the findings of

the project report for the betterment of the people of Ladakh.

Statement of the Problem

We propose to elaborately study the standpoint of Ladakh in the regional divergence of the state of Jammu & Kashmir; the question of Ladakhi identity and the issue of relative deprivation; demands for more political autonomy; the grant of tribal status to Ladakhis and the post-status mindset; status and performance of Ladakh Autonomous Hill Development Council; the impact of globalisation on socio-economic, political, and cultural life; the environmental concern among Ladakhis, emerging patterns of development and the discontent among the marginalized people.

Conceptual Framework

India is a state known for its diversity, be it social, cultural or communal. The state of Jammu and Kashmir represents India in miniature. In the development process of a state that envisages social, economic and political development, it has to carry forward the wheels of development to every part of its territory and people and if it fails to do so there are chances of people getting estranged from the state system followed by exhibition of discontent and annoyance. The problem further aggravates if the people affected have socio-cultural and ethnic distinctivity too. The same is true about the people of Ladakh in the state of Jammu and Kashmir. Today the process of globalization has brought about miraculous transformation in the life of people everywhere and the state of Jammu & Kashmir is no exception. The impact can be seen in the region of Ladakh too.

There is a changed attitude of the people who now think more in terms of development like a global citizenry instead of sticking to age-old traditions and ways. This goes on to work upon the popular mind and attitude. The general perception of the people of Ladakh vis-à-vis the people of the other two regions of the state and also the inter-regional and intra-regional equations within the state—form the prime content of the current study. Globalization and its impact on the social, political and economic life of the people of Ladakh, the constitutional status of Ladakh vis-à-vis Jammu and Kashmir in the state, the sense of relative deprivation and the Ladakhi response to insurgency in the state, powers and position of Ladakh Autonomous Hill Council, political participation among Ladakhis, comparative analysis of the socio-economic and political developments in different regions of the state, different social and political alignments within Ladakh, Globalization and the post-globalization discourse in reference to regional developments in the state of Jammu & Kashmir, patterns of development and the discontent among the marginalized people in Ladakh form the broad conceptual outline of the study.

Research Questions/Statements

The research questions to be answered/addressed need to be unequivocally stated:

- To study the inter-regional pulls and the extent of acceptance of Ladakhi identity in the state
- Are Ladakhis satisfied with the current status of Scheduled Tribe ?
- Is Ladakh Autonomous Hill Council sufficient to the multi-faceted development of the region?
- Has the process of globalization affected the socio-politico-economic and cultural life of the people of Ladakh?

- Are Ladakhis nonchalant to the phenomenon of insurgency in the valley?
- Insurgency in the valley has wide impact over the life and opinion of the Ladakhis.
- Ladakhis still look for UT status as the best alternative for bringing peace, order and development in the region.
- The emerging patterns of development and the trends in social, economic, political and cultural life of Ladakhis.

Methodology

We have applied an amalgam of historical, descriptive, comparative, analytical (Document analysis, Episodic and Running record analysis, Policy analysis, and Content analysis) and statistical methods as per the need of the study. The content of the regional demands of Ladakh in media reports, journals and government documents; historical accounts of Ladakh in travelogues and volumes and government policies have been studied. The data has been collected from both primary and secondary sources. For primary data besides government documents, reports and constitution we have also collected data through interview schedule circulated among 200 respondents. For this purpose the area of the study has been duly delimited.

Universe of Study

The region of Ladakh consists of two districts of Leh and Kargil. Geographically Kargil is much smaller than the region of Leh but demographically the two regions are equipoised as the population of Leh and Kargil is 1,47,104 and 1,43,388 respectively.

Leh district, geographically the largest one in India, falls to the East of Kargil district in the Ladakh region of Jammu and Kashmir and is bordered by Sinkiang district of China in the North, Tibet in the East and Lahul-Spiti area of

Himachal Pradesh in the South. Both the districts of the region of Ladakh are characterized by high mountains with three parallel ranges of the Himalayas i.e. the Zanskar, the Ladakh and the Karakoram ranges. Between these ranges flow three rivers i.e. Shayok, Indus and Zanskar. A big majority of the population of the region live around the valleys and patches near these rivers. The district consists of nine blocks i.e Leh, Khaltsi, Kharu, Nyoma, Durbuk, Nubra, Chuchot, Saspol, and Panamic.

The district of Kargil has an area of 14036 square kilometers and it is surrounded by Kashmir, Kishtwar, Lahaul Spiti (Himachal Pradesh) and Gilgit-Baltistan (POK). It is situated in the lower river basin of Suru. Two more rivers converge here which are Drass and Wakha Chu. Kargil is the second biggest town in the region leaving behind Leh. It is almost situated at the mid-way between Srinagar-Leh National Highway. There are nine blocks in the district i.e. Kargil, Drass, Zanskar, Sankoo, Taisuru, Shargol, Shakra-Chitkan, GM Pore / Trespone and Lungnak.

The data has been collected from these two districts of Leh and Kargil. For the purpose of survey, a sample of 200 respondents was drawn from four blocks i.e. Leh, Nyoma, Kargil and Drass; two each from the districts of Leh and Kargil.

The sample is purposive to give due representation to different sections of the society i.e. gender, rural-urban, literate and illiterates. The male female ratio in the district of Leh is 55.40% and 44.60% while in Kargil it stands at 52.48% and 47.52%. The sample represents the facts broadly in the same proportion. The broad description of the sample is given below:

Table No. 1.3

Block-wise sample of the Research Survey conducted

District	Blocks	Respondents	M/F
Leh	1 Nyoma (Rural)	50	27/23
	2 Leh (Urban)	50	27/23
Kargil	1 Drass (Rural)	50	26/24
	2 Kargil (Urban)	50	26/24

Although the rural population of Leh district is 76% (24% urban) and of Kargil is 82.9% (17.1% urban) we have picked up the blocks on the rural and urban basis. The blocks of Kargil and Leh are urban while the blocks of Nyoma and Drass are rural. While the region of Ladakh is heterogeneous in character the districts are in contrast quite opposite i.e homogeneous in character. Leh is primarily a Buddhist majority district with about 85 % Budhists, Kargil is a Muslim majority area with about 80% Muslims. Due consideration has been given to communal character of these districts. The detailed profiles of the two districts together with the history, culture, society, economy and administrative and political structure of the region constitutes the following chapter of the study.

Notes and References

1 *Census of India,* 1971, p.11.

2 Harish K. Thakur, *Alienation and Integration in Jammu and Kashmir,* Jaipur: Alekh Publishers, 1999, p. 14-15.

3 *Census of India,* 2011.

Chapter 2

Ladakh: Land and the People

Perched on the shoulders of the Great Himalayas, Ladakh represents one of the highest inhabited places in the world. The land and the people of Ladakh have been a subject of interest for many. Over the centuries Ladakh remained at the crossroads of different cultures and religions thus paving the way for the evolution of quintessentially a unique culture of its own. Its significance owed primarily to the silk route conjunction that it provided to different people from Central Asia, Tibet, China and India. It remained an important trading centre for the moving caravans emanating from these regions. Here we present a broad profile of the region of Ladakh in a historical perspective. We will study in brief the history, geography, society, religion, customs, culture and economy of the region of Ladakh. The profiles of the two districts of Leh and Kargil with their administrative and political structure have also been discussed in order to delineate the problem.

Physiography of Ladakh

The region of Ladakh comprises of an area of 95,876 sq. kms. which is about 70% of the total territory of the state of Jammu and Kashmir. It is a large plateau that lies to the south of Karakoram range and is separated from the valley of Kashmir by the greater Himalayan range. From Kashmir it can be reached by crossing Zoji La Pass while from Manali it can be accessed by crossing passes like Rohtang, Baralacha and Tang Lang La. The town of Kargil is separated by Zoji La Pass from Kashmir and Fotu La Pass (Near Lamayuru) from Leh.

Ladakh, the northernmost region of the Indian state and the largest area within the State of Jammu and Kashmir in India has been known by different names in the past. It has been a region that conjoined the areas of Western China, Southern Russia, East of Iran and parts of North West India which now fall in the territories of Pak Occupied Kashmir. Broadly the region of Ladakh comprises of two districts of Leh and Kargil.

Ladakh is located between north latitude 30°452 to 35°502 and east longitude 75°452 and 80°312. It is bounded on the north and east by China, in the north-west by Gilgit and Skardu of Pak Occupied Kashmir, in the west by Srinagar, Baramullah and Anantnag districts of Jammu and Kashmir and in the south by state of Himachal Pradesh.

The average height of the region is about 12000 ft (about 3800 metres) with sharp variations of 8000 ft (about 2600 metres) in the district of Kargil to 20000 ft (about 6500 metres) in the high altitudes of Chang-Thang sub-division of Leh district. The main city of Leh is also located at a height of about 11500 ft. The geographical spread of Ladakh is like a vast expanse of land opening broadly from south-east towards north-west or west at the banks of river Indus.

This expanse or "trench doesn't descend below 10,000 ft or 11,000 ft of elevation.[1]

It is probably one of the highest inhabited lands of the world and life here simmers quintessentially like the one of frosty deserts. At a distance of 15 miles the hills and mountains here change their hue from golden brown to dark ruby, maroon brown, crystal grey, silver rock, black and many more. It is one of the astonishing wonderlands that offer startling magnificence and sterile barrenness at the same time. Its valleys and land spread like vast prairies and pasturelands with no sign of foliage and greens except the sand granules and granite soil.

The land here has to be made arable and fertile to extract the sprouts of life and sustenance. Lambert observed as early as in 1877 that "the prevailing features of this country are bare rocky mountains, bare grovel slopes, and bare sandy plains, with not a green thing, not a tree, not a bush, not even a blade of grass, excepting a grey kind of pricky sage crop here and there."[2] In the north the region is guarded by the high Karakoram Range that extends to northernmost territories of Pak Occupied Kashmir. "Ladakh is a land where earth and sky seem to meet and it looks like the roof of the world. It is a vast sandy desert full of gold granite dust and barren lofty mountains."[3]

The land that is of prime significance is the land of Central Ladakh or otherwise known as Indus valley. This valley is the chief life line of the region with Pangong lake in the east and Drass valley in the west. "Cultivation is being carried out at an elevation of 14000 ft. It consists of the great Himalayan mountain ranges—the Zanskar, the Ladakh, the Muztagh and the Kunlun, with heights varying from 17,000 ft to 23,000 ft. These ranges run from south-east to north-west, and in between the valleys of Indus,

Zanskar, Nubra, Drass and Shyok are located."[4]

The region of Ladakh feature some of the vast and most outstanding valleys, passes and rivers of the world. These valleys and passes bear some unique characteristics of their own and are world known for their marvels of past and present.

Nubra is the largest valley of the region with Nubra and Shyok rivers as its feeders. There are many more small rivulets and springs that water the valley. The valley which is about 128 miles long and 72 miles wide has an area of about 9216 square miles.[5] It is bounded by Karakoram range in the north and Kailash range in the south.

"As compared to the other parts of Ladakh, the Nubra valley is sufficiently warm and fertile. People grow apples, apricots, pear and grapes. Wheat, barley and peas are the main crops. Potatoes, cabbage, cauliflower and raddish are the main vegetables."[6] The valley is the prime source of grains, fruits and vegetables for the whole of the region. Leh lies at the northern bank of the river Indus. It forms Central Ladakh and is the major part of the Indus Valley that has an area of 4000 sq miles. This stretch of land is equally fertile as people grow fruits, vegetables and food grains in the valley.

Suru valley has a fascinating landscape. Its glaciated topography with steep gorges, cataracts, alluvial fans, river terraces and socio-cultural milieu have large potential for the explorers, trekkers, leisure seekers and academicians. It is towered over by the Nun-Kun peaks. The glacier beds of the Nun-Kun peaks caused the formation of the Suru river. At Penze river gets separated from the catchment of Zanskar by moving westward where it is joined by the Shafat Nallah on its left bank near the pastures of Gulmantango. Thus the total sprawl of the Suru valley is about 2900 sq miles.[7]

The other important valley of the region is the Zanskar Valley which has an average height of about 13,500 ft. and is spread over an area of 3000 sq miles. It is spread over the banks of Zanskar river and lies between the folds of Zanskar range in the north-east and the Himalayan range in the south-west. Nubra, Shyok, Suru and Zanskar are the main rivers of the region which lastly merge into the fold of Indus river, the prime river of the region.

Mountain Passes in Ladakh

Name of Pass	Height	Location
Karakoram	18550	Head of Shyok River
Saser	17,820	Between Nubra and Shyok rivers
Hanu	16700	Between Indus and Shyok rivers
Khardong	18,380	Between Leh and Nubra
Lazgung	17,500	Between Leh and Nubra
Changla	17,350	Between Indus and Long Kongma
Lanak La	18,100	Tsomoriri
Zoji La	11,300	Between Sonmarg and Drass, Kargil
Umasi La	17,370	Between Zanskar and Kishtwar
Kongta La	15,495	Between Long Kongma and Chushul
Senge	16,952	Between Zanskar and Lamayuru
Pangache	16,495	Zanskar
Fotu La	13,400	Between Leh and Kargil
Namiika	13,000	Between Leh and Kashmir
Pen-Cho-La	—	Between Kargil and Zanskar
Taglang La	17,500	South of Leh
Polokonka	16,300	Near Tsho-Kar
Nakpogund	18,000	North of Tsomoriri
Lunga Lacha	17,000	Between Zanskar and Rukchu
Bara Lacha	16,500	Between Lahul and Zanskar
Digar La	17,930	Between Digar and ...
Laecha	16,660	Kulu-Leh
Nira	16,000	Kishtwar-Kargil

Penze La	14,440	—
Botkol	14,370	Kishtwar-Kargil
Nidar	17,000	Chng-Thang
Birokla	—	Near Drass
Charkang	16,700	Between Lukung and Gunle
Charchar	16,300	Leh-Padum route
Chelang Labho	14,850	Near Zangla in Zanskar
Hinjo La	13,513	Between Wanla and Sumdah Valleys
Keptung Kiptung	17,642	Leh-Chang Chenmo route
Riberang La Sumdo	16,100	Between Markha and Kharnak
Shushal	16,954	Shushal to Nima Mud
Singhe La	16,600	Between Yelchung and Futtoksir

Source: *Alexander Cunningham , Ladakh: Physical, Statistical and Historical with Notices of the Surrounding Countries, New Delhi: Sagar Publications, 1977, pp. 164-65. Sumi D Tokan and op.cit. p.22, Gazetteer of Kashmir and Ladakh, 1890/1974*

People

Ladakh is inhabited by a mixture of races primarily Mons, Mongols, Aryan, Dards and Baltis. The migration into the region has taken place at different intervals and as early as the ancient civilisations were on the move. The evolution of Ladakh into a magnificent livable height attracted many central and north Asian tribes. Meyak, Do'ng, and Sme were the first popular nomadic groups that entered the region from the north of Indus valley and settled in Chang Thang sub-division of Leh district. Ladakh, holds Jina, derived its name Mar-yul after the settlement of these tribes in the following way:

Sme-dong ≥ Sme-rong
Sme-rong ≥ Sme-yul
Sme-yul ≥ Smang-yul

Smang-yul ≥ Mang-yul
Mang-yul ≥ Mar-yul

There are accounts about the visit of Hieun Tsang who passed through Ladakh in 629 AD. Hieun Tsang refers to two barren countries of Himalaya named 'Ko-hu-lo' and 'Ma-lo-so' the latter being referred to Ladakh.[8] According to Cunningham the 'Ma-lo-so' here seems to be mistaken for 'Ma-lo-po' or 'Mar-po' which is Ladakh.[9]

The people who first migrated to the region were Mons, a group that resided over the northern or north-eastern tract of Kashmir such as Zanskar. Mons are said to be residing in the country of Manus which was situated between Kullu and Lahul. Manus can be Monhali or Manali according to Abidin. However, there are more observations about the movement of Mons. Tibetan chronicles tell us that the home of Mons was 'Za-Zung' which comprised of Indus valley and its tributaries up to the borders of Dardistan. The whole of Za-Zung was not under single rule and was divisible into small principalities like states governed by 'Magspons'. So there is possibility of movement of certain tribes from the areas of Kullu, Manali, Lahul and Spiti into Ladakh which settled in the upper areas of Kashmir.[10] Chinese have given different interpretation to the move as they see the Mon settlement from the Barbayon of the Northern Tibet.

Dards were the next to migrate into the region. The broader settlement of the Dards could be found between Drass and Nimu of the region. Dards here occupied the cultivated lands in lower Ladakh. The rock carvings around Kha-La-che tell us that they arrived here somewhere in the second or the third century A.D. Dards living between Drass and Lamayuru were overwhelmed by Islam in the 15th century.

Mongols of Tibetan origin migrated from Central Tibet into Ladakh in the 9th century A.D. This happened during the reign of King Langdarma who persecuted and killed many Buddhist monks of Ladakh. Later after his death his son Skyid-Ide-Nyimagon conquered Western Tibet whose eldest son DPal-gyi-mgon got the share of whole of Ladakh from his father in 930 A.D. His domain extended from Ru-thog in the east to La-rtsa in the west and to Ser-Kha-gog-po (Serkha Gompa) in the north.[11]

Baltis, a brave people who successfully repelled Chinese incursions for centuries, the carriers of Buddhism and Aryan and Tibetan culture entered into the region in the 10th century A.D. "The Balti people are partly of the Tibetan stock, with considerable Caucasoid (Aryan) blood in their veins. They speak an ancient form of Tibetan language and share the same culture".[12]

Society, Religion and Economy

Buddhism has left an indelible impact on the society, culture and value system of the region. The people here are humane, compassionate, cooperative, hard working, hospitable and docile. Since Polyandry remained a strong tradition among Ladakhis for centuries the role of woman becomes significant compared to other societies. Woman here plays a pivotal role in family and social activities. We can relate few accounts of scholars here who visited the region in the past.

According to Marco Pallis who visited Ladakh in 1936, "the Muslim sisters whom we had met on the way, had looked worn and suspicious, but here we saw rosy complexions and unaverted eyes. The Ladakhi wife is anything but a doormate; more often than not, she is the real ruler in her home, and children, when asked about their parentage, will often give their mother's name before their father's".[13]Ganapat who visited Ladakh in 1928 says, "The Ladakhi lady is complete head of her household, and the men are well underneath her extremely capable thumb. She has her own money, she trades on her own, her words are very much law. And lastly, when she meets on the road side, she passes the time of a day cheerfully and freely, which is most attractive to anyone who has spent long years in the veil-cursed east".[14]

Although Buddhism is known for its egalitarian structure yet it has its own characteristics in Ladakh where it has developed a mixture of socio-economic classifications. There are Rgyal-Rigs (Royals); Sku-Drag (Nobles); Dmang-Rigs (common people) and Rigs-Man (Unclean or outcaste). This is visible from the broad classification that difference is exercised in social interaction and behaviour. However, while looking for Rinpoches, the incarnated Lamas, no such differentiation is exercised and they can be taken from any category mentioned above. The close aides of a Rinpoche search for his next birth usually by looking for the supernatural signs which reflect the area, place and conditions of his rebirth. It can be in the shape of identification of the articles or texts of previous life by a child, religious bent of child, incantation of religious mantras by a child, a dream by a devotee or kinsman of a deceased person, insistence by a child that he should be worshipped like a Lama and not fostered to play.

The Buddhists who undertake celibacy as a lifetime vow are called 'Gedun'. The males are called 'Lamas' while the females are named 'Ani' or 'Chomos'. The 'Lamas' reside at monasteries but if they break the 'sheela' or rules of Buddhism then they are supposed to stay outside the monastery. Those Lamas who chose to live a married life also stay outside the monastery. 'Chomos' on the other hand attend monastery only on certain functions. At some monasteries they congregate in the evening for prayers and disperse to the nearby nunneries meant for their residence. They are mostly engaged in the work of agriculture, growing of vegetables, keeping sheep flocks and cattle and do the irrigation work in the fields of the monasteries.[15]

Mons who are regarded as the first settlers in the region are placed at low rung of the social hierarchy. They receive an outcaste treatment in the social functions. They are made to sit at the outer circles and use their own saucers, cups and plates (or pieces of wood or cloth made for this purpose) for food in festivals and ceremonies. The higher class families do not take food prepared by them, do not sleep in their beddings, use their clothes or have sexual relations or they would be reduced to the lower ranks in the society. They were said to be the people who were invited by the kings of Ladakh for making music for them.

There is another category known as Beda which is placed even lower to the Mons in social ladder. They are musicians and beg for barley or any other eatable or money at door to door. Mostly they beat one sided leather drum called *Daff* to entertain people. This makes their livelihood and they don't have permanent settlements due to which they have earned the reputation of beggars. However, Francke holds that those Aryans who remained Buddhists were called Mons while those who converted to Islam were called Beda. But it is noticed that there are Beda people in both the Buddhist and Muslim communities and the division of Mons into two observed by Francke may not necessarily be right.[16]

The customs of Ladakh region have their own peculiarities and uniqueness. Evolved under the typical Ladakhi geo-spatial reality they attract the people around though many of them share commonality with the adjacent regions. Child birth is one of the significant social event. The Ladakhis on such ocassion would rely more on prayers and chanting than on medical facilities, of course because of dearth of such medical aid in the past. The father of the child is regarded as the main custodian of the child and has to keep up to his house for at least a month. During this internment his cooking and servings are also forbidden at social level. In case the father is away at such happening he won't be allowed to enter the house before the completion of a week. The father can't even enter a monastery for a month in either case. This custom is prevalent in other regions of J&K and Himachal also, of course with regional variances.

The marriage ceremony would involve the offerings in Chang or likewise drinks. First the parents of the boy would fetch a suitable girl for their son. This is followed by a visit by boy's uncle or *Phaspuns* with Chang pot to girls' family. They then offer the *Khatak* and Chang to the girl's parents and would let them know about the intention. If the response is positive then the continuous process of feasts begins i.e. *HolChang, Tee-Chang, Trabs-Chang, Nyen-Chang, Nyo-Chang* etc. During these ceremonies the responsibilities and liabilities of different parties regarding the marriage are settled.[17]

Then there are *Tarchoks* (flag like cloths of different colours) of red, blue, green, yellow and white colours which are imprinted with mantras with the help of wooden blocks. These *Tarchoks* are divinized by certain rites (Rabnas) of the Lamas and are hoisted at four corners of the houses to save them from evil spirits. They carry various kinds of mantras and are symbolic of love, affection, peace and security and even are posted at high altitudes and mountain tops.

In case of illness, the Lamas also act as medical practitioners since they are approached for the performance of *Storma-Phang-ches* ritual which is used to remove or remedy the suffering. This seems to be purely a traditional religious exercise and it involves no actual treatment from medical point of view. But now a days with the availability of medical facilities people do not go to the Lamas any longer.

The construction of new house requires purification of the land. This is done by the Lamas who are called from a monastery to perform the rites. The ceremony is known as *Jing-sReg* Ceremony. For the welfare of all the members of family the rituals are performed by Lamas. This is called *Chos-ton*. The Lamas numbering between 3 to 30 are invited according to the capacity of the family head. On such occasions the Lamas read *Bum* or *Kangyur* and *sTangyur* and are given Rs. 50 to 100 per day.

The death ceremony popularly called *Sheston* is again a ceremony of significance. More Lamas join in case the affected party is economically sound and vice-versa. The ceremony prolongs in the case of former and may take a week's time. Rites are performed by the Lamas and usually son carries the body of the parent. Since the region is dry and bereft of vegetation, the people here burn the dead in a stone or brick chimney called *Spurgam*.

Ladakhi is the main language of Kargil and Ladakh regions yet it shares a common history with the language spoken in Baltistan. The joint inheritance of the Ladakhi and Balti owes to the branch of Western Tibetan family of languages together with Purukiri and Zanskari. The two regions of Ladakh and Baltistan together formed the part of Yarlung Dynasty of Tibet in 7th and 8th century. It was during this period that Tibetan script (yi-ge) evolved.

However, with the advent of Islam, the Baltis left the script in favour of Persian or Arabic since they considered the former to be of Buddhist origin.[18] Today the people of both the region understand Ladakhi and Hindi though, Bodhi or Ladakhi is the main language of the region of Leh and Balti and Urdu of Kargil region. There is a demand these days for the induction of Ladakhi (Bhoti) in the 8th Schedule of the Constitution of India.

Religion

Although the religious character of Ladakh has undergone a fundamental change yet a majority of the people here are Buddhists living in Leh district and Zanskar block of Kargil district. Zanskar has become important source that throws light on the advent of Buddhism in the region. According to Zanskar inscriptions Buddhism entered Ladakh somewhere around 2300 years back or third century B.C. Buddhist missionaries of Ashoka were instrumental in the spread of Buddhism. However, Mons were the first to come over the region and embrace Buddhism. Consequently with the help of Mons Buddhism expanded rapidly in the region and even beyond it. However, Hui Ch'ao's account reveals that Buddhism reached Ladakh much before it reached Tibet. In 747 A.D. the famous Buddhist scholar and Monk Padama Sambhav went to Tibet and established first order of *Lamas* or monks and it was after this that Buddhism spread to the other parts of Tibet and around.

Here it would be significant to count upon what Pervez Dewan observes:

"We also have evidences that in ancient times Kashmir used to be a flourishing centre of Buddhism. We further know that the eleventh or twelfth century murals on the walls of the Alchi monastery are the creation of the Kashmiri painters. These murals alone in all of Ladakh are purely Indian with no Tibetan influence. Pre-Tibetan Buddhist rock engravings can be seen near Drass and Zanskar. At Mulbek, next to the highway, and in Kartse Khar are sculpture of Bodhi Sattva Maitreya (eighth century A.D.). These carvings are in much deeper relief than those of the post-Tibetan period. So Buddhism reached Ladakh possibly in first century A.D. and certainly by the second. It is equally certain that it came through Kashmir, even though a millennium later Tibetan Buddism would overwhelm the indigenous society".[19]

Therefore, the advent of Buddhism in Ladakh seems to have been around one or two centuries before or after Christ. Since the kingdom of Kanishka, a Buddhist expanded up to Kashmir he came to be the chief patron of the religion in 2nd century A.D. In this regard it is significant to consider Francke:

"Buddhism got such firm hold in Kashmir that the fourth Legendary Council under King Kanishka (125-152 A.D.) is said to have been held at Jalandhara in Kashmir. Either after the third or the fourth Council Buddhism must have been carried to Western Tibet, situated between Kashmir and Yarkand. And as the case of the Mons shows plainly, the mission cannot have been a religious mission only, it was apparently a civilising and colonising mission as well. It would have been difficult to influence the wandering nomads without founding centres of Buddhist teaching with temples and monasteries. The almost empty land attracted more colonies, and the religious settlements grew into villages and towns in course of time". [20]

Over the millennium there were several political and social uproarings leaving the region to the aggressors, missionaries and sages. In 6th century A.D. Ladakh passed into the hands of Tibetans but Lalitaditya, a famous king from Kashmir defeated the Tibetans who kept on raiding Kashmir time and again. But since Lalitaditya found it difficult to control this horrid zone Ladakh mostly enjoyed a great deal of freedom till 822 A.D. when Tibetan king Lang Dar Ma was assassinated for his anti-Buddhist postures and his attempts to exterminate Buddhism from his kingdom. After assassination his sons Tashi Tsegspal and Skitde Nemagon took shelter in Tsang and Purang provinces. The latter founded the Ladakh Dynasty and expanded his kingdom up to Baltistan (in Pak Occupied Kashmir) and Lahul and Spiti now in Himachal Pradesh. It is believed that in the same period the Mongols of Tibetan origin settled down on the upper portion of Ladakh. They consequently spread the Buddhism of Tibet which is of Mahayan cult.

There was a tradition among the people of Ladakh to send their monks to Tibet for higher learning. This tradition continued till 1950 when China occupied Tibet and the Buddhist clergy was thrown out. Even today Ladakhi Buddhist prefer to get higher learning at Lhasa, if possible.

The other significant religion of the region is Islam. It is on records that Rinchin Shah, son of king Morup Gon of Ladakh had some conflict with his father, hence he was forced to run to Kashmir. He did a remarkable job there and ascended to the throne of Kashmir with the Islamic name (given by saint Bulbul Shah) of Sadarud-din-Rinchen Shah. He is said to have the credit of first Muslim king of Kashmir where he ruled for three years. Hence, he happened to be the first to embrace Islam and the message reached Ladakh.

Another important event in connection with the

expansion of Islam was the migration of two Nyathistani princes of Suru Kartsey to Kashmir and their conversion to Islam (1345-1400). Since the two had access to the king of Kashmir because of some highly dedicated work done, the king of Kashmir got his daughter married to one of them named Rgyalbum Ldey and bestowed them with a potential army and region beyond Chattergal as dowry. The two brothers reconquered Suru Kartsey and restored their rule. They also brought some Akhons and preachers from Kashmir and spread Islam in the Purig area. Since Rgyalbum Ldey was from a royal family, his conversion to Islam had a long lasting effect on the people of the area. They made their capital at Pashkum and later shifted to Mulbek. They got several mosques built in different areas of the region. The Khachay Masjid of Mulbek is considered to be the oldest mosque of the Ladakh region. Even today we can see the graves of Mosolu Begum, Rgyalbum Ldey and Chosbum Ldey at Mulbek.[21]

The other important event is when Sultan Shihab-ud-din (1350-1375) of Shah Miri dynasty of Kashmir invaded Ladakh and Baltistan again and extended his empire to these states. During the time of Sultan Sikander Khan(1394-1416 AD) Ladakh and Baltistan were again brought under control. This was followed by Zain-ul-Abidin's invasion of Ladakh in 1451 and 1470 that gradually forced the Ladakhis to convert to Islam. During the period of Sultan Sayed of Kashgar an army under the command of Mirza Haider Dughlat was sent to invade Ladakh from north. The commander entered Nubra and plundered the residents and also forced them to embrace Islam. Those who resisted were killed.

Islam was further strengthened in Ladakh by Mongols in 1532 under the command of Mirza Haider. Later on after

50 years king Jamyang Naamgyal was defeated by Ali Mir and he was compelled to give shelter to Islam in Ladakh. During his period rebel chiefs of lower Ladakh refused to follow his orders. To give them lesson he invaded their territories. But when he entered in Baltistan, the Balti ruler Ali Mir defeated him, and forced him to marry his daughter Gyal Khatun. Later with the help of queen Gyal Khatun many muslim Baltis arrived in Ladakh. In this way with the support of queen Gyal Khatun Islam further got chance to strengthen its roots in Ladakh.[22]

Gradually, in the centuries to come the transformation of the Valley into Muslim majority region also in one way or the other helped Islam spread beyond the region. It primarily encompassed the adjacent regions of north-west Jammu and north-west Ladakh. Today there are many Muslim monuments in Ladakh. Major among them are Imam Barah, Chushot Gongma, Masjide-e-Sharif Chushot, Gongma, Imam Barah Chushot Yokma, Khanqah, Chushot Yokma, Masjide-e-Sharif and Imam Barah, Thicksay, Masjide-e-Sharif Ahle-Sunnat Thiksay, Masjide-e- Sarif, Shay Yokma, Imamia Jama Masjid Leh, Imam Barah Leh, Jama Masjid Ahle-Sunnat Leh, Masjide-e-Shah Hamdan, Shay, Imam Barah and Masjide-e-Sharif, Chogso Phyang, Masjide-e-Sharif, Bogdang, Masjide-e-Sharif Diksit, Masjide-e-Sharif Partapur, Masjide-e-Sharif, Masjide-e-Sharif Achinathang, Hunder Mosque, Bazo Mosque, Tyakshi Mosque and Turuk Mosque.

Important Muslim festivals are Id-ul-Fitr and Id-ul-Zuha celebrated by both Shia and Sunnis. They also celebrate Id-ul-Milad-un-Nabi (SAW) and Milad-e-Ali (AS) on 12th rabi-ul-Awwal and 13th of Rajab respectively at Leh itself. The Shia Muslims also celebrate Id-ul-Gadeer. Shia Muslims also celebrate Moharram at all the Imam Barahs in Leh, Diksit,

Nubra, Hundar, Partpur, Turtuk, Tyakshi and Bogdang. These Majlis and festivals of the area keep all the Muslims aware of their religious principles, teachings Hadith, morals and ethical values so essential for communal harmony and brotherhood. Similarly Yum-e-Hussaini and Nawroz are also celebrated in the region.[23]

Economy

Since Leh constituted an important post on the erstwhile silk route, it acquired over the centuries a significant position so far as trade centre. It acquired the identity of one of the main markets (Mandi) of the central Asian trade, the other being Tibet, Yarkand, Kashmir and Turkistan. The region of Ladakh which has 35,237 hectares of land (3.42 p.c. of the state of Jammu and Kashmir) is primarily one time cultivable crop land. The cultivable land here is largely spread around rivers, streams and watersheds and is found in patches - small and big. Due to inclement weather for over half a year most of the crops are sown once a year. The land is broadly spread at the elevation between 9,000 to 14,500 feet above the sea level.

The major products of the region are barley, wheat, grim, pulses, peas and vegetables like cabbages, potatoes and radish etc. Regarding fruits, the land offers fruits like apple, apricot, plum and citrus which are found in plenty. Kargil is famous for its yields in cabbage, cauliflower, tomato, potato, turnip, knolkhol, etc. while Nubra valley is famous for its apricot, chulley and oil. Grim, also known as Zan is a staple food of the region and is used in multifarious ways like tea, roasted form and even for brewing. Live stock that mainly comprises of goat, sheep, yak, cows, dzos etc. is another important part of the economy of the region.

The bazaars of Leh and Kargil offer a glittering look ranging from the age old items like shawls, pashmina, tweed, wool, brassware, shoes, carpets, rugs, Buddha idols, manis, paintings, pieces of sculptor, silver chains and ornaments to items of modern electronics, cotton jeans, antiques, factory ware and packed food items. Kargil is rich in mineral wealth also as copper, sulphur, limestone, borax, chromite, soda etc.[24]

In industrial front Ladakh has not much to boast. Tourism industry is the main bone of Ladakh which in turn is highly scattered over the vast lands of Ladakh. The popular tourist places are Kargil, Drass, Leh, Padum, Zanskar, Nubra, Chanlang, Choglumsar, Thicksey, Zangla, Suru Valley, Shyok Valley, Sankoo, Rangdung etc. The roads are largely maintained by Government of India and increased transport and communication facilities are set to improve the economy of the region.

District of Leh

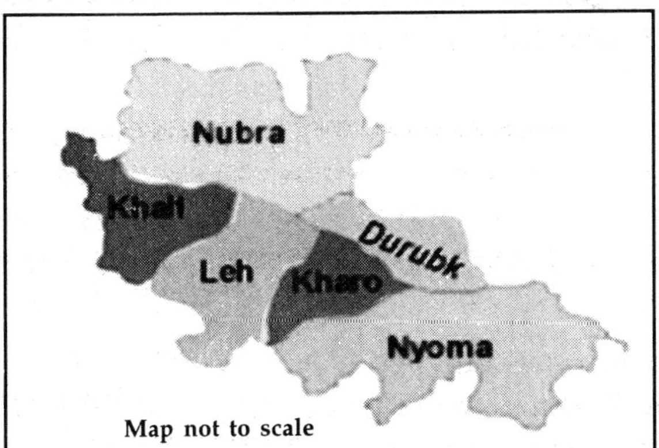

Leh that has a geographical area of 45110 sq. kms. is the largest district of India so far as area is concerned. However, its small population also makes it the first district to have lowest population density in the country. The district of Leh borders, 'Pak Occupied Kashmir' and 'China Occupied Kashmir' to the north and north-west respectively. Lahaul and Spiti district of Himachal Pradesh lies to the south of Leh whereas Tibet to the east. This northernmost ridge of the Indian sub-continent lies at an elevation of 2300 meters to 5000 meters between 32° to 36° north latitude and 75° to 80° east latitude. It is the coldest and the most elevated inhabitation in the country.

Three rivers, Indus, Shyok and Zanskar run through three mountain ranges of the region and the inhabitations largely concentrate in their valleys. Leh is situated at the bank of river Indus. The temperature of Leh oscillates between two extremes of 30° degree Celsius in the summer to minus 35° degree Celsius in the winters.

There are many tourist places in the district of Leh. The nine storeyed Leh Palace is one of the main attractions of Leh. It was built in seventeenth century by a famous ruler of Ladakh Sengge Namgyal. At a distance of 70 kms from Leh is situated the Gompa of Alchi. It is built on the banks of river Indus. The gompa is said to be about thousand years old and is looked after by monks of Likir Monastery. Another important palace which was the seat of pre-Tibetan kings is at Shey about 15 kms north of Leh. In palace is installed a 7.5 metre tall copper statue of Lord Buddha. It is also plated with gold and is considered the only one of its kind.

In the heart of Leh town is Jama Masjid which was built in 1666-67 after an understanding between Mughal Emperor Aurangzeb and the ruler of Ladakh Deldan Namgyal. About 19 kms. from Leh is Thikse Monastery. This monastery is famous for architectural beauty and has exquisite images, stupas and wall paintings of Lord Buddha. Phiyang monastery is 17 kms. from Leh at Leh-Kargil

National Highway. Built in 16th century by Tashi Namgyal, the gompa belongs to the Red Cap sect of Buddhists. Inside the gompa are kept hundreds of icons and idols of Lord Buddha on wooden shelves and chiffons. At the top of a hillock at a distance of 8 kms. from Leh is the Gompa of Spituk. It was built in 15th century and has many Buddha icons and five thankas. It also houses a collection of ancient masks, antique arms and an impressive image of Mahakal.

There are many fairs and festivals in Ladakh. Annual festivals of Gompas take place in winter because it is a time when people are less busy with work. During the festivals dramas, dances and mask dances are performed which represent various regions' heads and gurus. The largest of these monastic festivals is Hemis that is celebrated in June-July every year in dedication to Padam Sambhava. Other festivals held in summers are of Lamayuru in July, Phyang in late July, Tak Thok after Phiyang and Karsha in Zanskar after Phiyang. The monasteries of Spituk, Thiksey, Chemreay and Matho have their festivals in winter.

Administratively the district of Leh has three subdivisions viz. Nubra, Changthang and Khaltsi; three tehsils Leh Khaltsi and Sumoor; and nine blocks as mentioned in Table No 2.1 viz. Leh, Khaltsi, Chuchot, Nubra, Kharu, Saspol, Nyoma, Panamic and Durbok.

Politically, the region of Ladakh has one Parliamentary seat and two State Assembly seats of Leh and Kargil. At district level it is governed by Ladakh Autonomous Hill Development Council, Leh consisting of 30 Councillors (26 elected and 4 nominated). It is headed by Chairman Chief Executive Councillor (equal to State Cabinet Minister) who is assisted by four executive councillors. The council works according to the 1995 LADC Act., Constitution of Jammu and Kashmir and Constitution of India.

Table 2.1

S. No.	Leh District	
	Blocks	**Tehsils**
1.	Leh	1. Leh
2.	Kaltsi	2. Khaltsi
3.	Chuchot	3. Sumoor
4.	Nubra	
5.	Durbok	
6.	Kharu	
7.	Saspol	
8.	Nyoma	
9.	Panamic	

District of Kargil

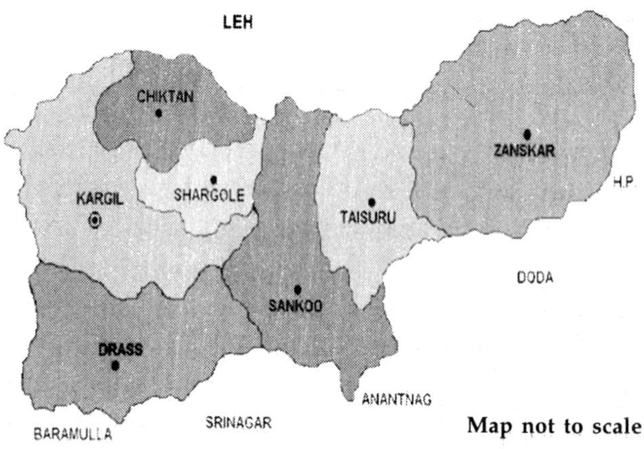

Map not to scale

The district of Kargil was made in July 1979 by the then Sheikh Abdullah government. It has a geographical territory of 14036 sq kms. which was sliced out of the erstwhile Ladakh district. Situated at the north-east of Kashmir Valley at a distance of 205 kms. and to the west of Leh at a distance of 235 kms. Kargil constitutes an important part of Ladakh mid-point halt at the Srinagar Leh National Highway. To the north-west Kargil borders Pakistan.

The district has a high altitude areas ranging from 8000 ft. to 18,000 ft. This is the reason that 99 % of the population here has been declared as scheduled tribe. Kargil district remains cut off from the rest of the country from November to May every year because of heavy snow fall at National Highway near Zoji La Pass, the highest peak in the region.

Politically it is represented in Parliament by a composite seat of Ladakh whereas at state level Kargil has one assembly seat. Administratively the district of Kargil has three subdivisions viz. Zanskar, Kargil and Drass; three Tehsils viz Kargil, Sankoo and Zanskar and nine blocks as mentioned in Table No 2.2. viz. Kargil, Sankoo, Taisuru, Shargol, Shakr-Chiktan, Zanskar, G.M. Pore/Trespone, Drass amd Lungnak.

Table No. 2.2

Kargil District	
Blocks	**Tehsils**
1 Kargil	1 Kargil
2 Sankoo	2 Sankoo
3 Taisuru	3 Zanskar
4 Shargol	
5 Shakr-Chiktan	
6 Zanskar	
7 GM Pore/Trespone	
8 Drass	
9 Lungnak.	

Politically the district is governed by Ladakh Autonomous Hill Development Council, Kargil consisting of 30 Councillors (26 elected and 4 nominated). It is headed by Chairman Chief Executive Councillor (equal to State Cabinet Minister) who is assisted by four Executive Councillors. The Council works according to the 1995 LADC Act., Constitution of Jammu and Kashmir and Constitution of India.

A good majority of people (about 94.7 %) reside in rural areas and only 5.3 percent people live in towns. Majority of the people here are Muslims. Total cultivated land stands at around 10,000 hectares as against the reported area of 19,437 hectares. The soil is generally coarse, a compound of gravels and stones. It is alkaline in reaction and organic matter content is very low. The fertility of the soil varies from place to place and the growing season is short. The average rainfall in Kargil is 26 mm. which creates an adverse situation for agriculture.

The district of Kargil represents a composite culture of Balti, Ladakhi, Purki, Dardi, Zanskari and Shia cultures. However, leaving aside the diversity conveyed by their varied identities almost all the people speak Kargali with ease. The district has one of the oldest civilizations comprising of tribes like Dards and Baltis. The latter are said to be descendants of the Saka tribe of central Asia. Dards are mostly concentrated in Drass area. There is an old stone statue near Drass which tells about the people and the land. General Zorawar Singh also constructed a fort at Kargil while his expedition of conquering the area through Warwan Pass.

Zanskar and Suru Valley are the main attractions for the tourists in the region. Expeditions for Nun-Kun mainly take off from Panikhar village here which is the base for the long treks to Kishtwar and Kashmir. Zanskar is another important destination for the tourists and Padum is the centre for hard but rewarding treks to Manali of Himachal Pradesh. There is also a small hermitage of Dzonkhul on way to Umsai La. Statue of Lord Chamba at Wakha Mulbek and a monastery on the top of hill rock at Shargole are the other important places in Kargil.

Notes and References

1 *Gazetteer of Kashmir and Ladakh,* New Delhi, Vivek Publishing House, 1890/1974, pp.9-10.

2 Cowley Lambert, *Trip to Cashmer and Ladakh,* London : 1877.

3 Sumi D. Tokan, Masato Oki and Fida M. Hassnain, *Ladakh the Moonland,* New Delhi: Light and Life Pub. Co.,1975, pp.19.

4 Prem Singh Jina, *Ladakh: Land and People,* New Delhi: Indus Publishing Company, 2009, p.14.

5 *Socio-Economic Profile of J&K: 2009,* Directorate of Economics and Statistics, J&K, 2010.

6 Jina, *op.cit.* p. 1.

7 Hussain Majid, "Tourism in the Suru Valley: Prospects and Problems", in S.C. Singh, (Ed.), *Impact of Tourism on Mountain Environment,* Meerut: Research India Publications, 1989, p. 148-49.

8 Thomas Watters, *On Yuan Chwang's Travels in India, 629-645 A.D.,* Vol. I, p. 299

9 Alexander Cunningham, *op.cit.* p. 4.

10 For details see A.H. Francke, *op.cit.* p.8, Jina, *op.cit.* pp.104-111

11 Paldan Thubstan,, *A Brief Guide to the Buddhist Monasteries and Royal Castles of Ladakh,* 1976, p.3.

12 A. H. Francke, *A History of Ladakh,* New Delhi: Sterling Publishers, pp. 20-21

13 Marco Pallis, *Peaks and Lamas,* London: Castle & Company, 1939, p. 234.

14 See Jina, *op.cit.,* pp. 180-81.

15 For details see Shakspo, op.cit., pp. 159-65 and Diwan, *op.cit.,* pp. 387-89.

16 *Ibid.,* pp. 161-162.

17 Jina, *op.cit.* pp. 177-198.

18 *Ibid.*

19 Pervez Diwan, *Jammu, Kashmir and Ladakh,* New Delhi: Manas Publications, 2008, p. 61.

20 Francke, A. H., *Ladakh: The Mysterious Land,* New Delhi: Ess Ess Publications, 1980, p.21.

21 See Zain-ul-Abidin-Aabedi, *Emergence of Islam in Ladakh,* New Delhi: Atlantic Publishers, 2009, pp.1-7.

22 Jina, *op.cit.* p. 179.

23 Field Survey conducted to collect data regarding the current project ***Inter-regional Divergence in Jammu and Kashmir: A Study of Ladakh Region,*** see also *Socio-Economic Profile of J&K: 2009,* Directorate of Economics and Statistics, J&K, 2010.

24 *Ibid.*

Chapter 3

Inter-Regional Divergence in Jammu & Kashmir : A Historical Perspective

The movements for more autonomy, right of self-determination and even secession and the political mobilization of people for the attainment of any such objective on one ground or the other derive from the historical, cultural, ethnic or socio-economic contextualities within the bounds of which they surge. India is a country that represents one of the most acute diversity at social, cultural and religious levels. However, the political paradigm that it opted for meeting with this diversity has worked well over the years. This is partially because of its federal character that caters to the needs of the people by providing them with the sense of governance and responsibility. Politically Jammu and Kashmir represents an outstanding chapter of Indian federalism since it enjoys a special status under Article 370 of Indian Constitution.

Theories of governance establish that if you want to appease the people, go federal. Federalism is the most effective antidote to check the splintering of multiple of identities in a society. This in fact, becomes important to a society inhabited by people belonging to different stocks, castes, religions and languages. These lines of integrity or homogeneity among people, at times, violate the superficial geographical borders put up by states and here becomes the task more complex and daunting to most of the federations.

The things become more intractable when the voices of disagreement and dissatisfaction come forth against the federal arrangements. Most states of the Eastern Europe, Asia and Africa are allergic towards the idea of harmonizing the ethnic and communal groupings within the fold of federal institutions. In Western Europe, the French also feel uncomfortable with the idea while one of the classic example of federalism i.e. United States also hesitate to extend the idea to the district level for which there are demands in the standing. " When American experts recommend federalism for other countries, such as Iraq, it is the American model they usually have in mind : a federation in which internal boundaries intersect with rather than coincide with ethnic and national boundaries".[1]

The opposition is largely due to the apprehensions that the increase in the degree of autonomy or political power to the multiple ethnic groups might lead to the emergence of fissiparous tendencies. This in fact, has been the common experience of many of the states like the erstwhile communists states of USSR, Yugoslavia, Czechoslovakia and African states like Nigeria. However, the causes behind their failure are altogether different from those where federal institutions have sustained.

Although, many of the states have opted, though with utmost care, for federal form of governments, especially those faced with diversity within them, yet the kind of models they have evolved vary from one state to the other largely based on distinct characters from their societal compositions.

These include Switzerland, Nigeria, India, Canada, South Africa, Belgium, Spain, and Ethiopia etc. Each of these countries has developed its own ways and means to deal with the fact of multiple "nationalities" in one nation-state. In almost all of these cases the geographic divisions of the country mirror to some extent, the ethno-linguistic divisions. But many also recognize that the various ethnic and religious groups are not each confined to a delimited territory.[2]

The complexity often requires constitutional provisions that recognize the need to assure rights for diverse groups throughout the territory of the country and not merely in one region. Canada, to cite just one example, has provisions for both French and English education rights in all parts of the country, even though French speakers are in majority only in one province. Is it not surprising that the oft quoted unitary nature of United Kingdom opts for more devolution of powers and plans to form elected regional governments in its major regions like North East, North West (around Manchester and Liverpool) and Yorkshire. To ascertain this, a referendum is on the move. The most startling example provides India as democracy and federal institutions have taken firm roots in this country. India, the world's largest democracy, provides the most glaring example of 'ethno-federalism' or a 'people friendly federal model' that has wonderfully met the needs of its multiple communities.

"With the reversion of the colonial powers to their shells

after playing havoc with the territories they governed the taste of freedom by different ethnic groups enthralled their passion for more power, autonomy and even secession from the central governments. This phenomenon of minority assertion led to a spate of violent conflicts and armed struggles in many states. Consequently the pressure mounted on political systems and many of them failed in their struggle to survive as unified political units."[3] India was also faced with the same dilemma at the time of partition. An amputated geographical unit, feeble administration, communal animosities, ethnic tensions, vague ideologies and unsettled boundaries added to the problem. It was under these circumstances that India had to opt for a loose convenient yet cautious federal system. The ground work was well prepared before independence when the same thing was felt earlier when the Government of India Act 1935 was passed. The Constitution of India largely borrows from this Act.

After independence the need was felt to accommodate the peculiar traditions, experiences and requirements of the country. Not only was an elaborate political system created with speed but the democratic structure it established had been institutionalized in considerable details. This has been possible because of both agreements on fundamentals and continuing diffusion of these agreements in the generation that followed independence. Even as early as in 1928, the Motilal Nehru Committee had framed a complete draft spelling out the features of free India's polity. It recommended, among other things, a parliamentary form and federal structure of the government and an exhaustive list of fundamental rights. These recommendations found overwhelming support among the members of the constituent assembly in the late forties.

During the discussions, debates were largely avoided and viable compromises were sought out on fundamental provision such as the federal structure of the country, the importance of the judiciary in interpreting the constitution and the question of a proper balance between the personal liberties of the citizens and the integrity of the nation, between the right to property and the goal of socio-economic development; the extent of decentralization of power to lower levels of the polity, the question of special rights and privileges of the minorities, and so on and so forth.[4]

The centralizing tendency was there because of the explicit fears of divisive forces. It was the need of the hour to provide for a system that would cater to both, the need of keeping the state intact and also provide full and if not full, a great quantum of autonomy to the states.

So a queer system of double governance was devised that looked at its units with an egalitarian view and also paid special heed to the requirements of some units, which was to create a great debate in the times to come. Where the state of Jammu & Kashmir was given a special status under Article 370 (of course under special circumstances), the states of North East, Maharashtra and Gujarat were also placed in certain manners on a different footing. Not that these states (except J&K) were to share more powers but presumably because of the backwardness of the people of these areas certain scheduled areas and tribal areas were identified to be looked after specially. These protective measures of the Indian Constitution make it a special constitution so far as its federal structure is concerned.

Article 1(1) of the Constitution of India declares that "INDIA" that is "BHARAT" shall be a "Union of states". In describing India as a "Union of states", the drafting committee of the Constituent Assembly followed the language of the Preamble to the "British North America Act, 1867". It was done deliberately to explain that the Indian federation to be set up under the constitution would be of the Canadian type. Explaining the significance of the use of the expression of union instead of the expression "Federation" Dr. B. R. Ambedkar, the chairman of the drafting committee, said that the word was adopted to indicate two things viz. (a) "that the Indian federation is not the result of an agreement between the units it constituted of and (b) that the component units have no freedom to recede from the union so created." [5]

The discussion of Constituent Assembly held on this provision, contained in article 1, made it further clear that the term "Union" was used as symbolic of the determination of the assembly to maintain the unity of the country. The expression "Bharat" was adopted by the Constituent Assembly because the country was so known in ancient times. It was also pointed out in the assembly that the name "Bharat" could be traced to the most ancient literature of India and was the only name befitting the history and culture of the country.[6]

In short, Indian Constitution has not used the word "Federal" and it describes India a "union of states." But India still finds a place in the list of federal states because it possesses all the essential features of a federal system. India has a written constitution and there is a division of powers between the centre and the states. The Constitution in India is supreme law of the land. The procedure for amending the provisions of the constitution is both rigid and flexible. The constitution establishes a free and independent judiciary to decide disputes between the centre and the states. Some special measures of the constitution regarding the states of J&K and the North East, which some people call as measures of discrimination, are as follows:

The State of Jammu & Kashmir

The State of Jammu & Kashmir is a constituent state of the Indian Union. But, it enjoys a special status under constitution. The reason for the distinction largely owes to the history and political developments after Partition.

Under the Indian Independence Act 1947, each of the Indian states was given the freedom to accede to the Dominion of India or to the Dominion of Pakistan or to declare itself independent. The Maharaja of J&K opted for independence but soon after his declaration, the state of Jammu & Kashmir was attacked by Pakistani forces under the guise of tribals. To protect the state against Pakistani aggression, the Maharaja of Jammu and Kashmir sought help from India and offered to the Governor-General of India to accede to the Dominion of India. The Governor accepted the offer with certain stipulations on October 26, 1947. The Maharaja of Jammu and Kashmir signed an Instrument of Accession to accede to the Indian Dominion. The accession was accepted by the Government of India but subject to its confirmation by the people of State. The people of the state confirmed their accession to India through their Constituent Assembly on November 17, 1957. The State of Jammu & Kashmir was thus declared to be an integral part of Union of India.[7]

When on November 26, 1949, the Constitution of India was adopted, the future picture of the relationship between India and the State of Jammu and Kashmir was not clear. Under such circumstances, Article 370 was incorporated which enabled the Constitutional position of the State vis-à-vis the Union of India to be defined from time to time.[8]

Although the State of Jammu & Kashmir is a part of Indian Union as defined by Article 1 of the Constitution read with first schedule, its constitutional status differs in the following respects:

1. The state has its own Constitution drafted by its Constituent Assembly, and the State is governed under this Constitution.
2. The power of parliament to make laws for the State of Jammu and Kashmir is limited to —

I. Those matters in the Union list and the Concurrent list, which in consultation with the government of the State, are declared by the President to correspond to matters, specified in the Instrument of Accession .

II. Such other matters in the state list, as with the concurrence of the government of the state, the President may by order specify.

III. Such other provisions of the constitution shall apply to that state, subject to such exceptions and modifications, as the President may by order specify.

But no such order which relates to matters specified in the Instrument of Accession referred to in paragraph 2 (I) above [Paragraph (I) of sub clause (b) of clause (I) of Article 370] shall be issued without consultation with the government of that State, and no order which relates to matters other than those specified in the Instrument of Accession, shall be issued without the concurrence of that Government. It thus follows that Article 370 empowers the President to define the constitutional relationship of that State in term of the provisions of the Indian Constitution, however, subject to the stipulation that:–

The President can do so with reference to matters in the Instrument of Accession in Consultation with the State Government and with reference to other matters, with the concurrence of the State-Government.[9]

It has been held that the President has power to vary, amend or modify a constitutional provision in any way he deems necessary, while applying it to that State. Articles 370 empowers the President to modify a constitutional provision not only when it is applied to that State for the first time, but he may subsequently also make amendments or modifications in such order earlier issued. Article 370 that has been inserted in the Indian Constitution to meet the demands of Kashmiris for more autonomy on the basis of which the state of J&K acceded to India has been greatly diluted. The Constitution of India provides for the application of different terms and conditions to different States. There is no constitutional guarantee of equality of treatment of all the States under the Indian Constitution. Hence the departure made in the case of Jammu & Kashmir in the distribution of powers is not a violation of the principle "equality before law".

Moreover, the State which is heterogeneous in character has been placed under a Unitary Constitution which was implemented in 1956. The constitution that the State adopted has built in provisions for the inter-regional tensions within the state. It is assumed that nothing threatens the unity of a heterogeneous people more than a unitary constitution.[10] Thus the regional realities of socio-cultural divergence were never dealt rationally by the constitution since it never devolved powers to the three regions of Jammu, Kashmir and Ladakh. The feeling of power centre hovering around Valley thus strengthened and paved the way for conflict within the State. Nurtured by ethno-regional feelings and cultural heterogeneity, the regional tension thus affected the political process in the state in the same fashion as the state has done at the national level. The state has become compartmentalized into three regions with none of them willing to exist under the dominant other two. This has bred the feeling of alienation among the Ladakhis at the one hand and Kashmiris and Jammuites at the other.[11]

Inter-regional Tensions

The inter-regional tensions have inflicted severe harms on the political developments of the state. "In fact, the politics in the State has been mainly based on two issues - the relationship between the Valley and the Centre on the one hand, and the relationship between the Valley and Ladakh and Jammu on the other "[12] Hari Ram characterises the politics of Valley as "politics of privilege", politics of Jammu as "Politics of Integration" and politics of Ladakh as "Politics of Isolation". Hence, socio-geographical differentiation configured different kinds of 'pulls' and 'pushes'.[13]

In the eighties also the sharp edges of the ethno regional dissimilarities continued to damage the composite cultural fibre of the state. The appointment of Wazir Commission on November 12, 1981 to look into the regional question also met the same fate as did happen with its predecessors. The Commission recommended the creation of three more districts in the Jammu region - Kishtwar, Samba and Riasi and one in Kashmir region i.e. Bandipore. The recommendations which mostly remained in favour of Jammu region remained unimplemented till 2007, though they were made as far back as on January 3, 1984.[14]

In 1987 the region of Jammu witnessed a great upheaval when the Farooq Abdullah's Government decided to turn Srinagar into a permanent capital of the state. The famous 'Darbar Issue' rocked the Jammu region when on October 7, 1987 Farooq declared that 29 departments would no longer be shifted to Jammu every winter.[15] (Jammu and Srinagar are the winter and summer capitals of the State respectively and the whole secretariat is moved to these capitals biannually). A series of strikes, bandhs and demonstrations erupted immediately. The lead was taken by the Bar Association which struck work in courts on October 10. The Muslim dominated towns of Poonch, Rajauri and Akhnoor also responded to the call of the Bar Association and observed a bandh on October 16.[16] The move was also criticised in Ladakh as in winters many of the Ladakhi leaders and people prefer to shift to Jammu.

So great was the public pressure that even leaders of the Congress(I), an ally of Farooq's National Conference, including MPs Janakraj Gupta and Girdhari Lal Dogra joined opposition leaders in condemning the move. Their attitude softened only after Farooq announced that 20 other departments would be permanently located at Jammu.[17] The intensity of the resentment could be judged from the shocking incidents of violence, looting of shops, stoning and ransacking of scores of Government buildings and arsoning and hundreds of agitators were locked up.[18] Joint Action Committee controlled by Bar Association was formed to oppose the move of the government. Its constituents were the BJP, Shiv Sena, Janata Party and International Democratic Front a Youth Organization. Except these, Muslim Action Committee (MAC) and Awami National Conference (ANC) were also represented by JAC.[19] In the light of about five week long strike and vehement resistance, Farooq dropped the idea later on after consultations with the central leaders. Following this the Bar Association withdrew the agitation on November 14, 1987, [20] but this led to the launching of another agitation by the Srinagar Bar Association against the new order of the Government that had annulled its previous move of permanently settling 27 of State Government departments in Srinagar.[21] But the call for indefinite bandh given by the Association that also turned violent in the valley didn't evoke much response from the people as MUF was opposed to it.[22]

Though, the 'Durbar Issue' ultimately came to be settled by reverting to the conventional practice of biannual movement of durbar, a practice being observed since 1870, the conflicting overtures of the three regions once again made it crystal clear that how great was the sensitivity of the regions towards each other. In fact, the 'Durbar Issue' became only an instrument of opposition to the Kashmir based leadership for the people of Jammu and Ladakh.

Though, the agitation ended after five weeks, it left a trail of bitterness, and caused a lot of tension between the regions of the state and became a matter of concern at the national level. Parochialism gained potency. Regionalism touched deeper cords and revived old memories of the Praja Parishad agitation in Jammu. Even a demand for a separate state of Jammu began to be made seriously.[23] The Kushak Bakula's LBA and its agenda came to the forefront with the voices for different alternatives lingering at the horizon. Similarly, Riasi also went into news when agitations erupted in the city demanding a separate Riasi District as had been recommended by a Commission headed by retired Chief Justice of J & K High Court, J.N. Wazir in January 1984. The agitation characterised by hartals, bandhs, and dharnas continued for about two months where after some assurances given by the State Government the agitation was withdrawn.[24] However, the discontent among the people of Riasi, Kishtwar and Samba remained prevalent as the recommendations of Wazir Commission still stand unimplemented.

Simultaneously, the discontent among Ladakhis has also been expressed from time to time by the people of the region. Ladakh Buddhist Association (LBA) is the chief organisation that represents the popular grievances of the region. LBA is more a cultural organization that aims at achieving the status of an Autonomous Hill Council for the region. Ladakh first raised the demand for NEFA type administration way back in 1962. When it proved of no avail, they called for greater regional autonomy in 1968. Four years later they started agitating for UT status, and finally in 1982, reverted to the demand for greater regional autonomy.[25]

LBA laments that although Ladakh has suffered discrimination all along 42 years since independence, it became more visible after Sheikh Abdullah returned to power in 1975. A political schism was surreptiously created which resulted in the formation of Leh and Kargil into two separate districts. The political fallout of this was tremendous for Sheikh. He succeeded in securing the sympathies and therefore, the votes of Kargil, hitherto diehard Congress supporters. The motive was far more serious than mere political expediency. It was meant to stifle a distinct Buddhist culture. By separating Kargil from Leh, Sheikh in a way conveyed the message to the Kargilites—predominantly Shia Muslims, that historical and cultural ties are insignificant factors in the Islamic polity he sought to impose on the State. This policy of divide and rule was carried further by Sheikh's successor Farooq.[26]

Ladakhis have a brimful pot of woes. In October, 1989, Ladakhis had not a single representative in 30 member Farooq Government. It has only two members in the State Legislative Assembly, though, it is larger in size than Jammu and Kashmir put together. 95 to 98 percent students fail to qualify in the matriculation examination due to the state's biased language and education policies. The whole of Ladakh does not have a single degree college. Ladakh was bifurcated into Shia dominated Kargil and Buddhist dominated Leh. Of the four Ladakhi members in the State's Legislative bodies as many as three are Muslims. The 86 percent Buddhists of Ladakh share 40 percent of jobs, while 12 percent Muslims have cornered 39 percent of jobs. Finally, while conversion to Islam is encouraged by State government, voluntary reconversion from Islam is discouraged through resort to brutal police repression.[27]

The economic policies of the State Government have also been bitterly criticized. If the State Government can give subsidy to the fruit growers in Kashmir, it should also provide some assistance to the vegetable growers of Ladakh who are surviving against the most formidable odds. The power sector despite figuring on the priority list, is a sad pointer to the State Government's non-performance attitude. Micro Hydel projects at Basgo, Summer and Hunder are yet to be commissioned, although work on these projects began ten years ago. Work on Domkhar Hydel Project and Igoo, the Irrigation projects that had the potential of changing the face of Ladakh, has been suspended. The Nimmie-Chilling Markha road suffered a similar fate due to the indifferent attitude of the State Government. Similarly, Leh was also left out of Border Area Development Programme despite its strategic position on Indo-Pak and Sino-Indian border.[28] The role of J & K Armed Police has also been described as discriminatory by LBA leader P. Namgyal. Its unwarranted intrusion into private houses and places of religious worship and ruthless repression of popular grievances has alienated the Ladakhis greatly.[29]

The demand for UT status was withdrawn by LBA in October, 1989 when President of India promulgated Constitutional (J&K) ST Orders on October 7, 1989 under Section A 341(1) of Indian Constitution. Scheduled Tribe status was granted to eight communities e.g. Balti, Beda, Bot, Bolo, Bropk, Dropka, Dard, Skin, Changpa, Corra, Mon and Puriyapa that covered 87.71 per cent of the population of Leh and Kargil districts. The decision was welcomed by LBA and it withdrew its long agitation for UT status.[30]

Hence, the Buddhists of Ladakh, especially of Leh District have felt being accorded step motherly treatment and their educational, administrative, and economic needs being deliberately ignored by the State Government. To counter such developments Ladakhis have kept their pressures on both Centre and the State authorities which, in consequence, has strained the relations between the Kashmir and Ladakh regions.

On the contrary, the NC leaders to keep their foot now intact in the valley have been using the 'Jammu Card' to bolster up their own leadership in the valley.[31] For instance the vicious communal propaganda launched by NC on the eve of elections, the introduction of the Resettlement Bill in 1982 and the Darbar Issue of 1987 reveal the intensions of the ruling NC party to rouse the regional feelings to perpetuate its own position in the Valley. The creation of these new districts in the valley while ignoring Jammuites also laid credentials to this policy of the Kashmiri leaders. Likewise, some political leaders have also been using the 'Kashmir card' in Jammu to gain ascendency in this region. The role of rightist organizations like BJP, Shiv Sena and RSS and students of ABVP has contributed to communalise the situation and thus alienate the Kashmiris.

Moreover, the State which is heterogeneous in character has been put under a Unitary Constitution. "The Unitary Constitution that the State adopted in 1956, had built-in provision for the inter-regional tensions. For nothing threatens unity of a heterogeneous people more than a

Unitary Constitution".[32] Thus the growing conflict within the state nurtured by ethno-regional feelings and cultural heterogeneity has affected the political process in the state in the same fashion as the state has affected at the national echelon. The state has become compartmentalized into three regions with none of them willing to exist under the dominating role of the other. This has bred the feeling of separatehood among Kashmiris as well as the Jammuites and Ladakhis.[33]

Religion and Language

The impact of religion on politics needs no elaboration. Historically, one finds that in India the pattern of interaction between religion and politics has varied from time to time and it has varied social consequences. In other words, religion was never able to fully extricate itself from politics nor could politics ever rid itself of religion.[34]

The history of the State of Jammu and Kashmir is replete with instances when the forces of religion worked hard on the inhabitants of Valley and Ladakh. The advent of Islam transformed the Hindu character of the Valley, both through force as well as will. It also spread to adjacent regions of Jammu and Buddhist majority Ladakh. However, the religious practices followed over the centuries in these regions didn't give way to the complete assimilation into Islamic culture and the state represents a mixture of culture that bear a uniqueness of Hindu, Buddhist and Islamic elements.

In the seventies and eighties several developments in the region played fire with the religious sentiments of the people. Following the onset of Iranian Revolution and the reactions to the Soviet Unions' aggression of Afghanistan, Muslim sentiment in South Asia underwent a profound transformation. A new kind of Islamic militancy emerged, and "there is no doubt about the powerful presence of the Islamic factor in Kashmir."[35] Islamic fundamentalism is a phenomenon which is understood very inadequately. Suffice it to mention that such ideologies batten upon the frustration of the under privileged classes which modernization has created in so many Islamic communities. While the frustration may be understandable, it often assumes a form of violent aggression.[36]

Since the early 1980s, a number of Muslim countries, most prominent of them being Pakistan, have been pouring substantial funds into Kashmir to create a network of fundamentalist missionaries in the valley.[37] The vicious communal propaganda launched by Jamaat-run-institutions which were banned by Jagmohan in March 1990,[38] has helped cultivating communal detachment in the valley. There is an important link between religion and nationalism which is stronger than connection between language and nationalism.[39] This religious base of nationalism that has become a popular outcry in the valley has provided an additional momentum to the forces of separatism. The religious ground on which Pakistan was created as a nation has its own attractions for Kashmiris as the latter have not only religious but also cultural, geographical and lingual bases to consider themselves as a separate nationality. However, the impact of this development in the Valley has created more fissures in different regions of the state.

It is interesting to note that strengthening of such nationalist forces on the basis of religion or community counter-strengthen the similar kind of forces present and this is the unwelcome development in the state. The presence of rightist Hindu organizations in Jammu and Ladakhi organizations looking for separate statehood or Union Territory status in Ladakh speak of the development.

To take the case of J&K state, as we have broadly taken the four major religions (Hinduism, Islam, Budhism and Sikhism) in Table No.3.1, majority of the population of the State 64.19 per cent. profess faith in Islam followed by Hindus 32.24 per cent, Sikhs 1.80 per cent, and Buddhists 1.16 per cent. This presents a picture that the state is not a homogeneous unit regarding religious faith. Muslims are concentrated mainly in the Kashmir region where they comprise about 95.35 per cent of the total population of the six districts of the region.

Table No. 3.1

Followers of major Religions in J & K , 1981 & 2001

Districts	Muslims		Hindus		Sikhs		Buddhists	
	1981	2001	1981	2001	1981	2001	1981	2001
Anantnag	95.64	98.49	3.77	0.99	0.59	0.47	--	--
Pulwama	95.88	97.60	2.50	0.93	1.63	1.34	--	--
Srinagar	90.65	94.65	8.39	4.06	0.89	1.07	0.02	
Badgam	95.94	98.07	2.63	1.03	1.40	0.84	--	--
Baramulla	96.50	97.55	2.02	1,29	1.46	1.03	--	--
Kapubara	97.53	97.36	2.02	1.95	0.44	0.53	--	--
Kargil	77.90	80.43	2.26	4.30	0.23	--	19.71	14.98
Leh	15.32	13.78	2.99	8.16	0.27	--	81.42	77.29
Doda	57.30	57.91	42.22	41.45	0.20	0.28	--	--
Udhampur	26.23	25.56	72.20	72.97	1.27	1.03	--	--
Kathua	6.96	8.14	91.16	89.79	1.65	1.66	--	--
Jammu	4.27	5.68	87.37	86.02	7.64	7.39	--	--
Rajauri	58.28	60.22	39.24	37.27	2.42	2.40	--	--
Poonch	89.06	91.92	7.29	5.20	3.63	2.76	--	--
J & K State	64.19		32.24			1.16		

Source : Census of India 1981, Series 8, J & K Census Atlas, Part - XII, Census of India, 2001.

The second largest community is of Hindus who are about 3.55 per cent followed by Sikhs 1.07 per cent. In the six districts of Jammu region Hindus are the largest religious community constituting about 56.58 per cent of the total population of the region. They are followed by Muslims,

40.36 per cent and Sikhs 2.31 per cent. Whereas all the districts of the Kashmir region with the exception of Srinagar have more than 95 per cent of Muslim population, only three districts of Jammu region Udhampur, Kathua and Jammu have Hindus in majority constituting 72.20, 91.16 and 86.37 per cent respectively. The other three districts Doda, Rajauri and Poonch have Muslims in majority who are 57.30, 58.38 and 89.06 respectively in percentage. In Kashmir region the district of Srinagar has 90 per cent of Muslims followed by 8.39 per cent of Hindus.[40] Majority of the Muslims in the valley belong to Sunnah sect. Budhists are mainly concentrated in Leh district of Ladakh region and comprise about 51 per cent of the population of the whole region. Muslims are the second largest community in this region concentrated mainly in Kargil and count for about 48 per cent of the population of the region. Most of the Muslims belong to Shia sect here.[41]

The decision of Sheikh Government in 1978 to give Kargil a separate district status had two aims, as would people from Leh interpret i.e. to divide the unity of Ladakhis which is essentially cultural and geographical. The purpose was to weaken the LBA movement for separate status and placate the Muslims of Kargil on communal lines, a preponderant majority in the area. The move worked and as the study goes (in the next chapter) it was noticed that as many as 74% respondents from Kargil district didn't opt for separate statehood or Union Territory status for Ladakh since they feel quite comfortable with the valley based leadership and would prefer to stay with Kashmir.

As regards the sense of marginalisation among Ladakhis vis-a-vis Kashmir and Jammu it has been noticed that there is a strong nexus between religion, culture and political aspirations. Firstly, this relationship becomes evident from the fact that Ladakh is culturally a homogeneous region strengthened by the reality that racially also they represent a distinct admixture of stock. This lends Ladakhis a distinctivity of their own and counterpoises them against the other two regions.

Language forms an important and sensitive medium of social interaction and communication in any area. It not only provides a platform for sharing common problems and concerns but also forms the most important vehicle of cultural progression. Since every culture has a specific value system it is only through the language that it progresses and pass on to the coming generations. A common language brings the people of diverse areas together and provides cohesion to the community by injecting a sense of oneness. In the prevalent situation the divisive role of language has also been witnessed by us in many states and regions and in the case of Ladakh also the role of language seems to have played a significant part.

As shown in Table No. 3.2 Kashmiri is the largest spoken language in the State followed by Dogri, Gojri, Pahari, Punjabi, Ladakhi, Hindi and Urdu. According to Census Report of 1981, Kashmiri language is spoken by about 89.49 per cent of population in the valley followed by Hindi which is spoken by about 8.49 per cent of the population. Hindi is spoken by the highest number of people in Kupwara (22.30 per cent) Baramulla (11.19 per cent), and Anantnag (7.39 per cent). The districts of Pulwama, Srinagar and Budgam have recorded 3.95 per cent, 3.28 and 2.84 per cent of Hindi speakers.[42] The figures regarding Punjabi, Ladakhi and Gojri are insignificant.

Gojri is the largest spoken language in the Jammu region which is spoken by about 54.50 per cent of people. Gojri,

Table 3.2
Principal Languages of the State
Persons speaking principal languages

Languages	Kashmir	Jammu	Ladakh	Total
Kashmiri	21,75,810	1,95,114	769	23,71,693
Dogri	8,161	1,30,845	----	11,39,006
Gojri	95,096	2,23,194	----	3,18,289
Pahari	51,065	1,95,377	----	2,46,442
Punjabi	45,890	1,12,005	523	1,58,418
Hindi	11,954	28,458	----	40,412
Urdu	4,521	7,057	----	11,578

Source : Census of India 1981.

Pahari, Punjabi and Hindi as shown in Table No. 3.2 are the other principal languages of the region.

In the region of Ladakh, Ladakhi is spoken by about 40 per cent of people followed by Balti (25 per cent). Dardi, Tibetan and the Budhi are the other principal languages.[43] However, the people of Ladakh (both Kargil and Leh) are having a good sense of understanding Hindi. Balti is more popular in Kargil district whereas Ladakhi is widely spoken in the district of Leh. It has been observed that these languages of the region have great similarities and almost all the Ladakhis are able to understand each other's dialects because of commonality of words.

The commonality of dialect with minor variations in the region of Ladakh is an important instrument of public communication and social interaction. It provides a substantial cohesive element to the society of Ladakh and has been the major instrument of mobilization of public opinion in the region. It is not only the religion (Buddhism), but more importantly the language that forms the distinct Ladakhi culture, rich heritage and provides sustenance to the idea of Ladakhi oneness and the regional aspiration of having a vision of separate state or Union Territory.

Literacy

Literacy is an important indicator of development at socio-economic level in a defined territory. It brings changes at the root level of the society and raises the consciousness level of the people and makes them aware of their interests of diverse kinds. The commonality of interests results in the formation of different interest groups which articulate demands and channel them in a democratic manner to the decision making machinery, a characteristic feature of modern civil society. But a society the members of which are mostly illiterate remains under the shackles of traditional and primordial loyalty structures. In such a society the people are generally apathetic towards the policy makers and hence a low consciousness level prevails that subject them to different pressures, both internal and external prevails.

A brief perusal of the growth of literacy in the state of Jammu and Kashmir as per Table No 3.3 shows that there has been a colossus increase in the rate of literacy in the last 50 years i.e. from 1961 to 2011. In 1961 the literacy rate of state was only 12.95 with a meagre rate of female literacy at 5.05 and male at 19.75. However, in 2011 the state has registered a growth of over 55 per cent with the rate of literacy at 68.74 per cent with female literacy at 58.01 and male literacy rate at 78.26.[44]

Table No 3.3

Literacy Rate 1961 - 2011			
	Literacy Rate		
Year	Persons	Males	Females
1961	12.95	19.75	5.05
1971	12.71	31.01	10.94
1981	33.02	44.55	19.86
1991	N.A	N.A	N.A
2001	55.52	66.60	43.00
2011	68.74	78.26	58.01

Note: - Literacy rate for the years 1961, 1971 & 1981 pertain to population aged 5 years and above. The literacy rate for the years 2001 and 2011 takes the population aged 7 years and above into consideration.

Table No. 3.4
Literacy Level

District/State	Literacy Percentage 1981			Literacy Percentage 2001		
	Persons	Males	Females	Persons	Males	Females
Anantnag	22.93	33.38	10.94	44.10	55.56	31.51
Srinagar	33.90	41.87	34.66	59.18	58.85	47.97
Baramulla	20.62	30.24	9.57	44.57	56.39	31.42
Leh	25.17	36.76	12.09	62.24	71.96	50.03
Doda	18.50	28.59	7.34	46.98	63.56	28.35
Udhampur	23.52	32.55	13.55	54.16	66.43	39.92
Jammu	42.86	52.60	32.24	77.30	84.92	68.75
Kathua	31.90	41.67	21.25	65.29	75.73	53.92
Rajauri	24.73	34.16	14.32	57.65	69.54	44.14
Poonch	23.39	34.20	11.24	51.07	65.41	35.30
Pulwama	20.47	30.56	09.21	47.76	59.24	35.40
Budgam	17.86	26.51	08.02	40.94	52.51	28.14
Kupwara	16.82	27.07	4.88	40.80	53.55	26.83
Kargli	18.86	32.26	3.14	58.21	73.58	40.96
State	26.67	36.29	15.88	55.50	66.60	43.00

Source : Census of India 1971, General Population Tables, and Census of India, 1981.

If we take literacy level of the three different regions of the state for the period from 1981 to 2001 as shown in Table no. 5.6, Ladakh, Jammu and Kashmir regions have registered 38.21 per cent, 31.26 per cent and 24.21 per cent of growth respectively. However, Jammu and Kashmir regions have lagged behind the region of Ladakh in the growth rate of literacy. Among districts of the Valley, Srinagar has the highest rate of literacy 59.18 per cent whereas Kupwara and Budgam stand at poor figures of 40.80 per cent and 40.95 per cent respectively. The districts of Leh and Kargil have shown immense growth as the two stand only behind Jammu district which has the highest rate of literacy at 77.30 per cent. [36]

Table No 3.5

Ranking of Districts by Literacy Rate and Sex 2011

	Persons		**Males**		**Females**	
Rank	District	Literacy Rate	District	Literacy Rate	District	Literacy Rate
1	Jammu	83.98	Jammu	89.77	Jammu	77.41
2	Samba	82.48	Samba	89.76	Samba	74.39
3	**Leh**	**80.48**	**Leh**	**89.39**	**Leh**	**64.52**
4	**Kargil**	**74.49**	**Kargil**	**86.73**	**Kargil**	**58.05**
5	Kathua	73.50	Kathua	81.40	Kathua	64.56
6	Srinagar	71.21	Srinagar	78.01	Srinagar	63.47
7	Udhampur	69.90	Udhampur	79.93	Udhampur	58.22
8	Punch	68.69	Punch	81.04	Punch	54.80
9	Rajouri	68.54	Rajouri	78.38	Rajouri	57.20
10	Baramula	66.93	Baramula	77.35	Baramula	55.01
11	Kupwara	66.92	Kupwara	77.10	Kupwara	54.79
12	Doda	65.97	Doda	80.36	Doda	50.34
13	Pulwama	65.00	Pulwama	75.41	Pulwama	53.81
14	Anantnag	64.32	Anantnag	74.13	Anantnag	54.15

15	Shupiyan	62.49	Shupiyan	71.86	Shupiyan	52.77
16	Kulgam	60.35	Kulgam	70.59	Kulgam	49.74
17	Ganderbal	59.99	Ganderbal	70.74	Ganderbal	47.62
18	Reasi	59.42	Reasi	69.93	Reasi	47.55
19	Kishtwar	58.54	Kishtwar	71.75	Kishtwar	44.13
20	Badgam	57.98	Badgam	68.18	Badgam	46.60
21	Bandipore	57.82	Bandipore	68.41	Bandipore	46.24
22	Ramban	56.90	Ramban	71.97	Ramban	40.04
	J & K	68.74	J & K	78.26	J & K	58.01

Source: Census of India, 2011

However, the figures derived from the Census Report 2011 present a more glaring picture as shown in Table No. 3.5. The districts of Leh and Kargil stand at third and fourth positions having literacy rate of 80.48 per cent and 74.49 per cent respectively. Jammu ranks first with 83.98 per cent of literacy and Ramban at the lowest rung with 56.90 per cent of literacy rate. If we take the region-wise statistics we find that the region of Ladakh leads the table with an average literacy rate of 77.48 per cent against the region of Jammu which has 68.79 per cent and Kashmir with 63.30 per cent respectively. The faster growth noticed in the region of Ladakh might be due to the fact that it is comparatively a less populated region with good educational institutions. However, keeping in mind the hard geographical terrains also the growth shows the wiliingness of the people to keep up with the requirements of the age as also about the high awareness of the inhabitants.

Up to 1989, there were 8835 primary, 2295 middle and 1184 secondary schools. Many new schools were also to be opened.[46] There were three universities and thirty four colleges. University of Kashmir had six constituent and fifteen affiliated colleges of Kashmir region.[47] The figures reveal that the strength of colleges (21) concentrated in the valley far outnumbered the colleges (13) located outside the valley i.e. in the region of Ladakh and Jammu. This has been one of the reason behind the sense of alienation among the people of Ladakh and Jammu.

However, as the Table No. 3.5 shows there has been a tremendous increase in the number of educational institutions in the state. There are in all 10540 Primary schools, 4991 Middle schools and 1785 Higher Secondary schools in the state (The data for the district of Anantnag is not available). The district of Udhampur has highest number of Primary schools (1190), Middle schools (574) and Higher Secondary/High schools (223). In the district of Leh, there are 214 Primary schools, 93 Middle schools and 39 Higher Secondary / High schools. Kargil has 226 Primary schools, 187 Middle schools and 49 Higher Secondary/High schools.

Although, the lowest number of educational institutions in the region of Ladakh can be attributed to the fact that it is a sparsely populated region but there is a glaring anomaly within the region of Ladakh. Leh which has more population (See Table No. 3.6) compared with the district of Kargil has much less number of Primary, Middle and Higher Secondary/High schools Although, there is a feasibility of geographical concentration working upon the development yet the lesser number of institutions in the district of Leh seem to be another reason that annoys the people of Leh who also see Kargilites now siding with the Valley.

Table No 3.6

Educational Institutions in Jammu and Kashmir (Schools) 2011

Districts	Primary	Middle	Hr. Secondary & High Schools
Anantnag	--	--	--
Badgam	584	320	100
Bandipora	446	164	48
Baramulla	873	422	135
Ganderbal	321	142	35
Kupwara	755	434	100
Kulgam	219	173	50
Pulwama	430	195	82
Shopian	251	77	27
Srinagar	252	136	49
Leh	**214**	**93**	**39**
Kargil	**226**	**187**	**49**
Doda	633	258	116
Jammu	765	266	158
Kathua	704	302	105
Kishtwar	330	127	56
Poonch	578	304	75
Rajouri	715	377	116
Ramban	345	121	45
Reasi	343	148	60
Samba	366	171	117
Udhampur	1190	574	223
Total	10540	4991	1785

Table No. 3.7

Educational Institutions in Jammu and Kashmir (Colleges) 2011

Institutions	Jammu	Kashmir	Ladakh	Total
Govt. Degree Colleges	35	35	2	72
Govt. Polytechnics	2	2	2	6
Pvt. B. Ed. Colleges	76	69	--	145
Pvt. Degree Colleges	13	3	--	16
Pvt. BCA Colleges	34	11	--	45
Pvt. BBA Colleges	27	5	--	32
Pvt. Law Colleges	17	6	--	33

As per Table No. 3.7 it is visible that the region of Ladakh has only two Government Colleges and two Government Polytechnics (one each in Leh and Kargil). Against this the region of Jammu and Kashmir are having 35 Government Colleges and 2 Government Polytechnics respectively. Besides this while Jammu region has 76 B.Ed. Colleges, 13 Pvt. Colleges, 34 Pvt. BCA Colleges, 27 Pvt. BBA Colleges and 17 Pvt. Law Colleges; the region of Kashmir has 69 B.Ed. Colleges, 3 Pvt. Colleges, 11 Pvt. BCA Colleges, 5 Pvt. BBA Colleges and 6 Pvt. Law Colleges. The institutional imbalance is quite visible here. The region of Ladakh has no such institution to its credit and the students have to move either to the Valley or to Jammu for higher education. The Adverse weather makes things difficult for Ladakhis. Hence, the non-availability of these institutions in the region of Ladakh definitely creates a bit of annoyance among the Ladakhis against the consecutive ruling regimes in the state.

A literally backward region is usually characterised by the existence of traditional and primordial institutions and its being at the earliest stage of transformation. The rate of political participation is low and the most of the people are apathetic towards the political institutions and the decision making process. In such a state the phenomena of interest articulation and aggregation is limited and interest articulation often takes place on communal or regional lines that might cause the conflicts and disagreements. A comparatively low level of literacy in Ladakh (though it has improved a lot now) and Kashmir region has its own repercussions on the evolution of regional distances within the regions. While it has fostered the sense of deprivation on account of development at the one hand, it has also emotionally charged the people of the regions against each other. However, the failure of the state governments to provide sufficient educational facilities to the people of Ladakh has also created a sense of nonchalance about the consecutive state regimes in the state.

Poverty and Unemployment

Employment generation is the most daunting task the states are faced with. The state of Jammu & Kashmir is one of those states which have lagged behind in generating employment. According to 1981 census there were only 30.37 per cent main workers against 55.74 per cent non-workers and 13.89 per cent of marginal workers.[48]

As the Table No 3.8 reveal the total number of main workers in the state of J & K were 18,18,570 out of which the region of Kashmir stands for the highest number of workers contributing 9,69,596 (53.32 per cent) followed by Jammu region's 7,89,282 (43.40 per cent) and Ladakh's

59,692 (3.28 per cent). If we take the percentage of the total main workers in regard to the total regional population, the region of Kashmir has an edge over the region of Jammu. The percentage of main workers in Kashmir region is about 31.00 against 29.31 in Jammu and 30.37 of the whole of the state. The region of Ladakh has 44.44 per cent of main workers.[49] However, the percentage of main workers in the region of Ladakh has suffered a decline to around 31 per cent as the Census Report of 2001 shows. This is still higher than the other two regions.

Majority of the main workers in the three regions of Ladakh, Jammu and Kashmir are engaged in cultivation. In the Ladakh region, 47778 persons are engaged in cultivation (20.06 %) followed by 2872 in agricultural labour and 1702 in house hold industry. A big portion of them is engaged in different jobs like live stock, forestry, tourism, transport, trade, commerce and small businesses etc.

In the region of Jammu 65.73 per cent of main workers are engaged in cultivation followed by 4.14 per cent in trade, 4.34 in livestock, 3.31 in agricultural labour, 3.25 in construction, 2.41 in transport, storage and communication, 2.27 in manufacturing processing, repair etc. and 0.21 in mining and quarrying. The region of Kashmir has comparatively less number of main workers engaged in cultivation (55.70) followed by 7.88 in manufacturing and processing, 5.67 in trade and commerce, 3.45 in agricultural labour, 2.81 in transport and communication and 2.01 in construction (See Table 3.8)

Table No. 3.8

Working Force (1981) Census

District	Total main workers (100.00 per cent)		Main workers as percentage of total population in the year	
			1981	2001
Anantnag	257131	135220	31.68	21.89
Pulwama	146585	61672	29.04	22.59
Srinagar	311052	53615	30.12	26.28
Badgam	154787	73795	32.81	24.48
Baramulla	267488	100295	31.43	22.93
Kupwara	111855	90018	30.37	17.48
Kargil	34205	17306	45.33	29.58
Leh	39841	19143	43.55	33.87
Doda	192636	124867	33.48	27.90
Udhampur	241950	121442	31.62	32.74
Kathua	158261	43943	28.82	29.08
Jammu	420865	94973	26.66	26.77
Rajauri	114429	100602	27.59	23.91
Poonch	85423	115474	27.72	22.99
Total J & K State	1818570		30.37	25.19

Source : Economic Review of J & K, 1990, Govt. of J & K : Directorate of Economics & Statistics, Planning & Development, 1991, p.48.

Table No. 3.9

Working Force : Number of Main Workers Engaged in Different Fields

Region	Cultivation	Agricultural labour	Live stock forestry, hunting etc.	Mining &Quarr ying	Manufacturing, processing, repairs, etc.	Construction Comm.	Trade & storage etc.	Transport & Comm.	Other services	Main workers as percentage of population
Kashmir	55.70	3.45	2.85	0.16	7.88	2.01	5.67	2.81	11.93	30.91
Ladakh	20.06	6.30	2.92	0.05	0.60	2.04	2.06	0.47	18.58	44.44
Jammu	65.73	3.31	4.34	0.21	2.27	3.25	4.14	2.41	12.01	29.31
J&K State	56.85	3.49	3.54	0.18	5.62	2.83	5.58	3.16	13.13	30.37

Source : Census of India, 1981.

Table No. 3.10

Working Force : Number of Main Workers Engaged in Different Fields

Regions	Cultivation	Agricultural Labour	Workers to Household industry	Other Workers
Kashmir	597174	175489	204188	786656
Ladakh	47778	2872	1702	57943
Jammu	954699	70026	23719	766833
J&K State	159651	248387	229602	1611432

* Main Workers refers to those workers who had worked for the major part of the reference period (i.e. 6 months or more) are termed as Main Workers. Marginal Workers are those workers who had not worked more than 6 months.

The data given above reveal that the Ladakh region has its main workers primarily engaged in cultivation, agricultural labour, livestock and forestry and other jobs. In Jammu region its working force is engaged mainly in cultivation, livestock and forestry, construction and trade and commerce. In the Kashmir region main workers are engaged chiefly in cultivation, manufacturing, processing and repair etc., trade and commerce, transportation and communication. Although the region of Kashmir share more than half of the total main workers of the state, less number of them are engaged in cultivation if compared to Ladakh and Jammu region. This is mainly due to non-availability of cultivable land and small size of per-capita landholding in the region of Kashmir (for more information see Table No. 3.10). The continuous squeezing of the land due to increased population has caused scarcity of work which has resulted unemployment and poverty.[50]

The same is true about Ladakh which is geographically the largest district of India. However, the availability of cultivable land in Ladakh is quite small and when a big chunk of main workers are dependent on cultivation the problem becomes more acute. Horticulture and tourism are the other two sectors which are providing necessary livlihood to the people of Ladakh but even tourism lasts for about 5 to 6 months only because the region gets cut off from the rest of the world for about 6 months.

A majority of people in the state, especially in the region of Ladakh and Kashmir, do not enjoy proper employment facilities that give rise to a poverty ridden class, a class that can grow unprecedented wrath and discontentment among the people. According to the census count of unemployed educated youth taken by the Directorate of Economics and Statistics J & K, the number of literate unemployed almost doubled from 0.36 lakh ending 1980-81 to 0.64 lakh ending 1986-87.[51] Assuming the same pace of annual growth during the later years the numbers should now be on the higher side of one lakh. The number of illiterate unemployed was even much greater as the literacy level in the state at that time was quite low i.e. 26.67.

The Employment Exchange data indicated a total of 1.25 lakh on the live register ending December 1989. There are 0.93 lakh literate unemployed and 0.32 lakh illiterate youth.[43] It is, however, to be borne in mind that only small numbers of unemployed educated youth get registered with employment exchanges and much less do the uneducated, because a very small number of placements take place through the exchanges and the state Public Service Commission and the Subordinate Services Selection Board does not necessarily recruit from the registered names in the Exchanges.

Agriculture, as shown in Table No.3.10, is the largest occupation that absorbs 60 per cent of total working force. However, since the total land under cultivation is very small (the per capita net area sown being less than 0.10 hectare and the average holding size not even one hectare) the capacity of the agriculture sector as an employment avenue has already exhausted.

If we take into consideration community-wise employment under State Government, Muslims who are a predominant community in the state constituting about 64.16 per cent of the total population share 57.67 per cent of the jobs (inclusive of gazetted, non-gazetted and inferior). Hindus who constitute about 32.24 per cent of the total state population share 36.59 per cent of the jobs.[53] However, the gazetted posts are sliced away by Hindus in much greater proportion to their total population in the state. Hindus share about 46.83 per cent of gazetted posts against 48.72 per cent by Muslims.[54] This is largely due to the appointment of IAS officers in the state from outside the state. In 1990 there were about 25 per cent state officers among IAS personnel. Out of 22 secretaries only five are Kashmiri Muslims. This is in violation of the agreement of 1958 between the State and Union Government that while extending IAS services to the state of J & K , the Centre would assure that 50 per cent of the posts would be promoted from the state services.[55] Again out of the total 14,743 persons employed by Centre as on January 1989, only 11.86 per cent of jobs are shared by Muslims if compared to 79.60 per cent by Hindus and 7.26 by Sikhs.[56] Buddhists who are about 1.16 per cent of the state population are in negligible number in the jobs. Thus there are reasons to believe the grievances of Ladakhis and Kashmiris that even in their own state they are not getting enough opportunities in state services.

Poverty and unemployment seem to be a major cause of annoyance among the youth. With the rise in literacy the people with rural backgrounds are no longer interested in earning their livelihood by farming and they want white collar jobs. Corruption has added to their resentment. Jammu and Kashmir gets ten times more financial assistance than the states equal to its size and population like Himachal and Punjab yet the development registered in the state is much less compared to other states. Ladakh region is not an industrialised one. The difficult terrains, inclement weather and poor transportation weaken the chances of investment in the region. This lessens the chances of employment generation also.

Power Generation

The state's potential (about 20,000 MW) to become self-reliant by exploiting water resources has remained limited since most of the projects here are controlled by NHPC. Power Development in Jammu and Kashmir has a long and distinguished history. 9 MW Mohra Hydro-Electric Plant, among the first of its kind in the subcontinent, was developed as early as 1905. Out of the total estimation of power generation in the state which is about 20,000 MW, the projects of about 16,200 MW capacities have already been identified. These projects are techno-economically viable, besides being eco-friendly and socially beneficial.

The state today is even faced with acute shortage of electricity. The shortage of power has not only restricted the growth of industries but has also put limits on the utilisation of capacity of the existing industrial units and lift irrigation schemes.

Peak demand in 1990 was estimated at about 600 MW and about 3,000 million units of energy. The availability, however, is much less and the balance is made up partially from the share available from the Central Project of Salal. In 1988-89, the import of power from outside was about 57 percent of the total availability.[57]

Important power projects in the state are Ganderbal 15.00 (MW), Upper Singh 22.60, Mohra 9.00, Lower Jhelum 105.00, Chenani 25.00,Gat Turbine 75.00, Bemina 5.00, Leh 6.00 and others 5.50. The new power projects that have been taken up are Third Phase of USHP II 35 (MW), Shitkari Kutan 84, Parnoj 37, Chenani II & III 6, Sewa II 6, Asthan Nallay 1, Kotan 0.75, Matchil 0.60, Lower Jhelum IV 36, Gat Turbine II 100 and Sewa III 120.[58] The key power projects are controlled by Delhi. During the rule of G.M. Shah, 400 KV transmission line was handed over to NHPC. The Sawal Kot and Baghlihar projects on the Chenab were handed over to NHPC during the first spell of Governor's Rule by Jagmohan in 1986 and 200 KV line project was handed over to NHPC in 1990 during his second spell.[59]

At present the NHPC has been entrusted seven projects in the state. These are 345 MW Salal stage I, 345 MW Salal Stage II, 390 MW Dulhasti, 450 MW Baghlihar , 600 MW Sawalkot, 480 MW Uri and 300 MW Kishanganga.[60] The Centre finalised an investment programme of Rs.8,000 crores for hydro-electric projects in the state during the 8th and 9th Five Year Plans.[61] Over the last decade, the power sector has been the major thrust area with an average of Rs. 100 crore spent every year, but the pumping in of such huge funds have not paid the expected dividends.[62] In the last three annual outlays of 1990-91-92-93 were spent Rs.192 crores, Rs.205 crores and Rs.250 crores respectively.[63] Thus with huge amount of money being invested in the power sector, the problem of non-availability of power in the state is likely to be diminished and that time is not away when the state would be able to export the power to other states.

The state government went a step ahead to benefit from the exploits in the field when it founded the Jammu & Kashmir State Power Development Corporation Limited (JKSPDCL) which was incorporated as private limited company on February 16, 1995. This would help extricate the state from the NHPC control and lends a sense of self-reliance as is there with most of the states in India. The Corporation was incorporated to takeover, execute, complete, operate and maintain all power stations and power projects of the State. The assets of all the power projects in the State, both existing and under implementation were transferred to the Corporation. The Corporation presently has 20 hydroelectric projects with installed capacity of 758.70 MW located in various districts of Jammu & Kashmir including 450MW BHEP.

The Corporation has Gas Turbines based on HSD with installed capacity of 175 MW at Pampore near Srinagar. In accordance with the State Hydel Policy, 2003 JKSPDC has allotted 10 small HEPs with a total capacity of 110.50 MWs under IPP phase-I. The State Government is presently reviewing existing State Hydel policy, 2003 for project implementation from 2-100MW to make it more investor friendly and thus attract investment and expertise from private players in the sector on a large scale. J & K State in one of its achievements took lead in award of a mega hydro power scheme on tariff based competitive bidding process. J & K is the first State in India to award 690 MW Ratle HEP (mega hydro power project) on BOOT basis through a tariff based competitive bidding process.

Table No 3.11

Power Generation Figures for 2010-11

S.No	Name of Power House	Installed capacity in MW	Net Energy supplied (Lus)
1	USHP-II Kangan	105	2910.29
2	Chenani-III Udhampur	7.50	72.68
3	Sewa-III H.E.P.	9	92.88
4	Baderwah Power House	1	0.00
5	Igo Mercellong MHP	3	105.26
6	Pahalgam MHP	3	78.78
7	Marpachoo HEP	0.75	9.78
8	Haftal	1	12.16
9	USHP-I Sumbal Kangan	22.6	337.98
10	Ganderbal Power House	15	117.49
11	Karnah MHP	2	18.98
12	L.J.H.P	105	3777.19
13	Chenani-I	23.30	717.15
14	Chenani-II	2	64.02
15	Iqbal MHP Kargil	3.75	81.35
16	Sumoor	0.10	0.66
17	Hunder MHP	0.40	5.89
18	Bazgo MHP	0.30	2.81
19	BHEP	450	28748.46
20	Stakna	4	4.65
	Total	758.7	37158.46

	Total Generation 2004-05		7322.93
	Total Generation 2005-06		8926.8
	Total Generation 2006-07		9527.64
	Total Generation 2007-08		8535.08
	Total Generation 2008-09		16981.732
	Total Generation 2009-10		34488.389

Source: http://www.jkspdc.nic.in/

Regarding the region of Ladakh the problem of power generation has been a daunting task. The state corporation is also pursuing the development of geothermal project in Pugah valley of Leh, Ladakh. There are in all nine projects in the region. As per Table No. 3.12, there are nine projects in operation i.e. Stakna (Leh), Iqbal (Kargil), Igo-Marcellong (Leh), Sanjak (Kargil), Haftal (Kargil), Hunder (Leh), Bazgo (Leh), Marpachoo (Kargil) and Sumoor (Leh). However, the projects have small output and the region look for larger projects in the future.[64]

Table No 3.12

Projects in Operation in Ladakh

Sr. No	Name of Project	Location	Capacity
1	Stakna	Leh	4.00
2	Iqbal	Kargil	3.75
3	Igo-Mercellong	Leh	3.00
4	Sanjak	Kargil	1.26
5	Haftal	Zanskar, Kargil	1.00
6	Hunder	Nobra, Leh	0.40
7	Bazgo	Leh	0.30
8	Marpachoo	Drass, Kargil	0.75
9	Sumoor	Nobra, Leh	0.10

There are several more explorations in the field of power generation in the region. In the Central Sector there is 45 MW Nimo Bazgo HEP on the river Indus and 44 MW Chutak HEP on the river Suru are at an advanced stage of completion. Against it in the state sector there are more projects in the way. Major among them are:

(i) 6 MW Dah SHP:- Originally estimated at 3 MW, the revised project report envisages harnessing potential of 6 MW by utilizing gross head of 279 meters. Work on this project is being commenced, with completion in 3-4 years time.

(ii) 5 MW Hanu SHP:- Hanu SHP has a revised capacity of 5 MWs, utilizing head of 234 meters. Work on this project is planned to start very shortly. It is expected to be commissioned in 4 years.

(iii) 0.500 MW Dumkhar MHP:- Work on this project had remained suspended since 90s owing to change in hydrology. This project is being completed for a reduced capacity of 0.500 MW, making use of the already constructed structures.

(iv) Rangdo SHP:- Prefeasibility report for 15 MW Rangdo SHP. has been prepared. This project will meet the energy needs of the Nobra valley.

(v) Tamasha Nallah SHP: Prefeasibility report of Tamasha Nallah SHP has been prepared for a capacity 8 MW. The project is located in Zanaskar Sub-Division of Kargil District.

(vi) Bairaas SHP: Prefeasibility report of Bairaas SHP has been prepared for a capacity of 11.5 MW. The project is located in Drass Sub-Division of Kargil District.

(vii) Pugah Geothermal: Technology Demonstration

Project (TDP) cum resource assessment project of 2-5 MW capacity is proposed to be set up in consultation with MNRE before steps for tapping the main reservoir are taken.[65]

J&K hydroelectric projects development policy 2011

A new hydel policy for expeditious development of hydro potential in the State and to bring in investment and associated efficiency of the private sector has been notified in July 2011. Identification of Projects to be bid out under the said policy is underway.

Therefore, in the power sector the region has a bright future as most of them are about to be completed in the next 5 to 8 years. This will not only meet the power requirements of the people but also increase the power revenue of the state corporation.

Investment in the state of Jammu and Kashmir by Delhi has been basically in two fields i.e. roads and communications for military purposes, both to suppress secessionist elements and to confront the border states of Pakistan and China. The objective is also to serve commercial purposes, power generation and transmission, so as to better exploit state's natural resources of water and forest.[66]

Thus, the State of Jammu & Kashmir is one of the less developed states as it lags behind other states in the field of industrialisation and agriculture. As a result the job opportunities have minimised and the unemployment has increased over the years. Increased control of the natural resources of the State by the Centre has also annoyed the people. Furthermore, the increase in literacy has also affected the job preferences of the people in favour of government jobs as against the traditional ways of livelihood.

Interest aggregation in developed states takes place on

economic lines whereas in underdeveloped states the interest aggregation takes place on narrow parochial lines like community, religion, caste, ethnicity etc. The migration of labour and the marketing of surplus products could cross the communal loyalties and pave the way for communal harmony. Putting in different words, a commercialised economy is a catalyst agent of increased social interaction and integrity. But the economy of the state of Jammu and Kashmir is at subsistence level. Thus the lack of economic development that fillip the poverty and unemployment is causative of alienation from the system in general and strained relations within the state in particular, a factor well found in case of insurgency in the valley.

Agriculture

The economy of almost all the developing and underdeveloped world has been dominated by agriculture. It is the only field that has been traditionally the single largest source of livelihood for the people. Agriculture has played the most significant role in the economy of the state of Jammu & Kashmir.

Agriculture, not only engages over 60 per cent of the main working force (see Table No. 3.10) directly but also the bulk of the marginal workers. It provides livelihood to thousands of other workers engaged in processing and distribution of the agricultural raw materials and products. Agriculture contributes half of the SDP and determines the upward and downward movement of the per capita income of the people.

Out of a total of 1.01 lakh hectares of total geographical area on this side of the LAC, 0.20 lakh hectare is covered by demarcated forests. 0.24 lakh hectare or 30 per cent is the only reported area under cultivation. The remaining 70 per cent is bare rock or desert mainly of Ladakh and Kargil region. The total area under plough viz. net area sown and current fallows is 8.22 lakh hectare or 10 per cent only of the total area not under demarcated forests. The cultivated area per capita for 1988-89 is thus 0.11 hectare only. The limited area under cultivation has led to the shrinking of the holding size and the average holding size, as per the agricultural census of 1980-81, is 0.99 hectare only. 70 per cent of the holdings are less than one hectare each in size. Holdings are fragmented and fragments scattered.[67]

Modern equipment and technology are making inroads into the agriculture but have a long distance to go. Tractorisation, chemical fertilizers and plant protection measures are very limited. 60 per cent of the sown area depends on rain and 47 per cent only of the net area is cultivated more than once. Productivity of land is low and little change discernible from year to year. Of the reported area, 29 per cent only is the net area sown and 34 per cent only the cultivated area. 27 per cent is occupied by undemarcated forests, 24 per cent is not available for cultivation and 14 per cent is under pastures, miscellaneous tree crops and culturable wastes.[68]

Over 80 per cent of the sown area is put under foodgrain cultivation which includes about 4 per cent under pulses. Maize is grown over largest area accounting for over 28 per cent of the sown area followed by rice with over 25 per cent and wheat with over 22 per cent of the area. Oilseeds occupy nearly 7 per cent, fruit and vegetables nearly 6 per cent, and fodder over 3 per cent of the sown area. Other crops are grown at very small scale and area less important except saffron which though small by area, is very important by the value it fetches.[69]

Up to March 1990, as the Table No.3.13 shows, the total number of landholders in the state are 10,35,336 who possess the landholdings (between 0.0 - 0.50 to 50.00 hectare and above) of about 10,29,557 hectares.

Table No. 3.13

Region-wise Landholders and Landholdings in the State of J & K

State/Regions	Number of Landholders	Landholdings in hectares (000)
J & K	10,35,376 (100 p.c.)	10,29,557
Kashmir	5,73,331 (55.37 p.c.)	4,03,348 (42.68)
Jammu	4,41,912 (42.68 p.c.)	5,90,972 (57.40)
Ladakh	20,133 (1.95 p.c.)	35,237 (3.42)

Source : Economic Review of J & K, 1990, op.cit., pp. 57-59.
See also: planningcommission.nic.in/plans/stateplan/sdr_jandk/sdr_jkch3a.pdf

Out of these the number of landholders of the Jammu region who are about 4,41,912 (42.68 per cent) possess 5,90,972 (57.40 per cent) hectares of land. In comparison to Jammu, number of landholders of Kashmir region who are about 5,73,331 (55.37 per cent) possess only 4,03,318 (42.68 per cent) hectares of land. The third region of Ladakh has 20,133 (1.95 per cent) landholders who own 35,237 (3.42 per cent) hectares of land.[70] Therefore, there is a visible difference in the possession of land by landholders of Jammu on the one side and Ladakh and Kashmir region on the other. The former possess greater share of land as compared to the latter. Although, this is largely due to the fact that Kashmir is the smallest region in respect of geography, whereas density of population is highest in this region. However, the lack of availability of cultivatable land to the people of Ladakh and Kashmir region provides an input to the economic underdevelopment as most the people are engaged in this sector.

The total irrigated land in the state (as Table No.3.14

shows) 3,02,601 hectare in 1980-81 increased to 3,09,813 hectare in 1985-86 and about 3.10 lakh hectare in 1988-89.[71] Out of this total irrigated land, Kashmir region had a better figure of 2,01,959 hectare against a meagre 89,246 hectare of irrigated land in Jammu region in 1984-85. Lack of irrigation facilities in some areas and climatic difficulties in others has restricted cropping intensity. Most of the cultivated area in the state, especially in the valley and the

Table No. 3.14

Total Irrigated Land

State/District	Irrigated area in Lakh hectares	
	Year 1980-81	Year 2001-02
Anantnag	0.46	0.78
Pulwama	0.36	0.58
Srinagar	0.18	0.22
Badgam	0.30	0.37
Baramulla	0.43	0.50
Kupwara	0.22	0.18
Leh	0.09	0.11
Kargail	0.08	0.10
Jammu	0.48	0.95
Doda	0.06	0.08
Udhampur	0.05	0.06
Rajauri	0.05	0.08
Poonch	0.03	0.07
Kathua	0.14	0.43
State	2.93	4.51

Source : Irrigation Statistics : 1985-86 to 2001-02[72]

region of Ladakh and the hilly districts of Jammu region, is put to a single crop only. Out of the net sown area of 7.03 lakh hectare during 1988-89, less than 3.30 lakh hectare (47 per cent) was sown more than once. In Jammu and Kathua districts almost whole of the net area sown, is sown more than once.[73] Since Ladakh region has less cultivable land as compared to the other two regions and the high altitudes make cultivation quite a difficult job, the area under irrigation here is nominal and statistically has got little to be construed. This in fact reduces the local food grain production and dependence on imports from outside the region.

Apple, pear, plum, cherry, orange, mango etc. are the important fruits of the state. According to the Revenue Department estimates, 0.46 lakh hectare was recorded under all kinds of fruits during 1989-90. The Horticulture Department have estimated the area for 1988-89 as 1.70 lakh hectares. The total production of fruit is anticipated to be of the order of 8 lakh tonnes and export during the year at 5.10 lakh tonnes.[74]

With militant violence choking tourism and transport, fruit production, farm production and handicrafts have become the major sources of employment in Kashmir. With 4.4 lakh families engaged and annual turnout increased to 300 crore rupees, horticulture has become the backbone of the state's economy. Fruit production has registered a 54 fold increase in the past four decades and the present production of 8.6 lakh tonnes is likely to increase further upto 14 lakh tonnes by the end of eighth five year plan.[75] Apple is the main crop with 6.21 lakh tonnes produced in 1991-92. Over 6 lakh tonnes of almonds, walnuts and other fruits were also produced during the same period. In this regard an Indo-Italian Project of Rs. 5 crore has been taken up at Ramban to promote olive cultivation and to extract oil which is a great foreign exchange earner. Similarly, Rs. 1.30 crore Indo-Bulgarian project has been taken up for improving the quality of apple. Another thrust area is to enhance the capacity of raising plants in nurseries. There are about 182 nurseries that raised about one lakh plants in the state in 1991-92.[76] Farm production, paddy cultivation in particular on which most of the people in the valley depend for their sustenance has continued as earlier.[77]

Roads

Roads and other means of communication such as telecommunications play a crucial role in transforming the economy of a society. The state of Jammu & Kashmir has undergone a remarkable change in this respect. The total road length (both surfaced and unsurfaced) in the state was 10,992 kms. in 1990 against 8,206 kms. in 1980-81. Despite the hilly terrain of the Kashmir region where road construction is an expensive task, the region of Kashmir enjoys a much better position than the other two regions.

As Table No.3.15 and Table No.3.16 shows, up to March 1990, the total road length in the six districts of Kashmir was 5,610 kms. (38.66 kms per 100 sq. kms.) against 4,056 kms. (21.16 kms per 100 sq.kms) in Jammu region and 1,366 kms. (3.00 kms per 100 sq.kms.) in Ladakh region. The six districts of the Kashmir region (Anantnag, Pulwama, Budgam, Srinagar, Baramulla and Kupwara) have a much better road network compared to the rest of the districts with the exception of Jammu and Kathua districts.

Table No. 3.15

Road Lengths in Various Districts of J & K State

Districts	Road Length per 100 kms. of area 1983-84	1989-90	Roads maintained by state PWD, kms. as per 1989-90 Report
Anantang	30.10	31	1238
Pulwama	51.79	54	756
Srinagar	36.54	42	931
Badgam	46.32	52	707
Baramulla	24.85	28	1298
Kupwara	23.37	25	680
Leh	1.28	2	782
Kargil	3.23	4	584
Jammu	40.91	47	1448
Udhampur	12.02	14	649
Kathua	23.54	25	674
Doda	5.36	7	773
Punch	7.47	9	151
Rajauri	13.46	15	461
Total			11132

Source : **Economic Review of J & K 1984-85,** and **1989-90,** Government of J & K, Directorate of Economics & Statistics, Planning & Development, 1986 & 1990.

In all the region of Kashmir has a greater length of roads as compared to the regions of Jammu and Ladakh, though geographically Kashmir is the smallest region. The region of Ladakh has quite little length of roads i.e. 1366 kms. However, over the decades the road length has almost doubled in the region. As per Table No. 3.16 the total road length of the state has increased from 11,132 kms. to 17,017.07 kms.

Table No. 3.16
Road Length, 2008

Districts	**Metal-led**	**Fair weather**	**Total**	**Road Length/ 100 sq. km.**
Anantnag	--	--	--	
Badgam	517.86	12.60	1230.06	89.71
Bandipora	84.60	--	251.1	63
Baramulla	1036	123	1973	47.09
Ganderbal	183	63	682	35.06
Kupwara	388	19.94	1119	54,,,,,,,
Kulgam	206.35	60.55	615	56.70
Pulwama	263.03	43.85	763.43	70
Shopian	176.23	--	445.18	72
Srinagar	194	82	1263	429.59
Leh	**149.65**	**688.76**	**1503.18**	**1.82**
Kargil	**406.85**	**448.22**	**1098.55**	**7.83**
Doda	135.62	54.67	364.8	10
Jammu	64.93	92.10	2384.42	76.99
Kathua	8	109	966	39.59
Kishtwar	28.78	97.78	218.01	16
Poonch	103.29	97.78	596.12	35.61
Rajouri	13.17	69.75	428.94	16.31
Ramban	56	37	169	14.88
Reasi	13	58.28	100.74	6.64
Samba	17.5	22.65	81.8	9
Udhampur	157.04	135.46	763.80	32.09

The region of Ladakh has registered twofold increase in road length which increases from 1366 kms. to 2601.73 kms. in 2008. However, the length of metalled roads is just 556.50 kms. in the region while fair weather roads are 1136.98 kms. Within the region of Ladakh, Kargil district enjoys the facility of more metalled roads (406.85 kms.) against a meagre (149.69 kms.) road length of Leh district which has more fair weather roads (688.76 kms.) against 448.22 kms. of Kargil district.[78]

Roads are the veins of economy and non-availability of all weather metalled roads in any region adversely affect the all round development of people. The same is true of Ladakh which is sparsely populated region with people settled far and wide. The people here have to stay in their particular zones for 4 to 6 months because of road blockages by snow at the higher peaks of the passes. Economically well off people, normally shift to Valley or Jammu in the winters and come back to Ladakh only in summers. Therefore, to revive the economy and fillip a boost in the commercial activities in the region, the construction of all weather roads, though, a costly affair (drilling of tunnels around high snow catching passes) is desirable. If China can extend its rail network to Lhasa why not Indian government can go for appropriate connectivity with Leh and Kargil, which from the defence point of view, is also required.

Table No. 3.17
Number of Post Offices in J & K (1985-86)

District	1983-84	1985-86	Area per P/O in 1986 (sq. kms.)
Anantnag	129	131	30.41
Pulwama	109	111	12.59
Srinagar	116	108	20.63
Budgam	55	52	26.36
Baramulla	152	157	29.22
Kupwara	66	61	39.00
Leh	44	44	319.00
Kargil	46	46	980.00
Jammu	189	189	16.39
Doda	119	121	96.62
Rajauri	120	121	21.74
Kathua	113	113	23.46
Poonch	44	44	38.05
Udhampur	154	154	29.55
J & K State	1454	1452	69.82

Source : Ibid., pp.74-75

Telecommunications and Health

A look at the telecommunications facilities in the state as shown in Table No. 3.17, according to the data available, reveals that up to 1986, the six districts of Kashmir region had a better coverage of area per post office which stood at 26.36 sq. kms. when compared to the State's coverage of 69.82 sq. kms. and of Jammu and Ladakh region's coverage of 37.63 and 649.50 sq. kms.respectively. However, the total number of P & T offices had risen from 1454 in 1986 to 1877 in 1989.[79] Though the region of Ladakh is geographically largest with little population yet the area coverage by post offices here is startlingly low, a matter of concern.

Table No. 3.18
Number of Medical Institutions (1985-86)

Region	District	No. of Medical Institution (1985-86)	Population per Med. Institution
Kashmir	Anantnag	172	4282
	Pulwama	99	4615
	Srinagar	116	6822
	Budgam	103	4150
	Baramulla	162	4715
	Kupwara	129	2868
Ladakh	**Leh**	**106**	**738**
	Kargil	**123**	**59**
Jammu	Jammu	193	3095
	Kathua	137	3095
	Udhampur	179	2906
	Rajauri	102	3484
	Doda	244	1937
	Poonch	78	3282
J & K State		1943	3499

Source : Indicators of Regional Development : 1985-86 (Govt. of J & K: Dir. of Eco. & Sta., Planning & Dev., 1987), p.67.

The availability of health facilities as specified in Table No. 3.18 indicate that out of 1943 medical institutions (inclusive of all Hospitals, dispensaries and primary health centres) in the state in 1986, the Jammu region had highest number of medical institutions i. e. 933 followed by Kashmir 781, and Ladakh 229. The number of people served by a single institution in the six districts of the valley is comparatively very high if we consider the figures of the other two regions. In 1989, there were 7556 hospital beds and 2788 doctors, haqims and vaids.[80] However, the lack of medical facilities in Kashmir region when compared to the other two regions provides a sense of discrimination among Kashmiris. However, as the Table No. 3.19 shows in 2008 there were in all 3517 health institutions (District Hospitals, Sub-District Hospitals, Primary Health Centres and others) in the state of Jammu and Kashmir. The region of Kashmir has about 1374 health institutions while the region of Jammu has in all 1842 health institutions. Though, the data regarding the district of Anantnag is not available yet the region of Jammu has higher number of institutions. Against it the region of Ladakh has in all 300 health institutions which indicates the availability of less number of institutions. But if we take the population coverage by the number of health institutions then since Ladakh region has quite small a population here a health institution is serving much lesser number of people than the two other regions.[72]

Table No. 3.19
Health Institutions, 2008

Districts	Distt. Hospital	Sub-Distt. Hospital	PHCs	Others
Anantnag	1	-	-	-
Badgam	1	9	36	168
Bandipora	-	6	9	99
Baramulla	1	8	32	247
Ganderbal	-	2	16	56
Kupwara	1	7	31	206
Kulgam	-	3	15	91
Pulwama	1	6	24	181
Shopian	1	2	9	75
Srinagar	1	1	2	26
Leh	1	2	14	124
Kargil	1	1	5	152
Doda	1	2	88	90
Jammu	2	8	43	363
Kathua	1	4	25	224
Kishtwar	1	1	7	74
Poonch	1	3	17	145
Rajouri	1	7	22	197
Ramban	-	1	49	39
Reasi	1	2	11	110
Samba	1	1	13	88
Udhampur	1	2	21	176
Total	19	78	489	2931

Source: Performance Review of Jammu and Kashmir 2008-09

Banks

The whole of the State of J &K has been brought under the network of various banks. As shown in the Table No.3.20 there has been an increase of 88 bank branches in the state between 1984 and March 1990. In March 1990, there were 746 bank branches in the State out of which the Jammu region shared 326 (43.70 per cent), Kashmir 398 (53 per cent) and Ladakh 22 (4.00 per cent). The dependency of population per branch was highest in Jammu which is about 72,553.

The banks have indicated a total deposit of Rs.1,53,923 lakhs ending March 1990. The deposits have shown increase of varying degrees during the years in all the districts of the state except Anantnag, Kargil and Kupwara in which decline has been -10 per cent, -9 per cent and -1 per cent respectively. There was a substantial decline of 25 per cent in advances during the last months of the year 1989 because of uncertainty and instability of law and order in the state. The decline was noticed mainly in Doda, Kathua, Anantnag and Srinagar districts. Srinagar was the worst hit district where 47 per cent of decline was noticed.[82]

Table No. 3.20
Area and Population Served by Bank Offices

District	No. of Branches Mar.1984	Avg.Dependence per branch. Area	sq.kms. Population	No.of Branches March, 1990	Avg. Dependence per Branch Population
Anantnag	53	8.05	13000	66	12258
Badgam	27	4.10	15000	33	14656
Baramulla	92	13.98	8000	106	8017
Srinagar	108	16.41	7000	112	7723
Pulwama	31	4.71	14000	32	15779
Kupwara	43	6.54	8000	49	8315
Kathua	41	6.23	10000	44	10788
Jammu	125	N A	N A	143	8328
Udhampur	43	6.54	11000	48	12111
Poonch	17	2.58	14000	36	15842
Doda	33	5.02	14000	36	14312
Rajauri	26	3.95	13000	37	10949
Leh	--	---	-----	**13**	**6714**
Kargil	---	---	-----	**09**	**8839**
State	658	100	10000	746	10107

Source: Economic Review of J & K 1984 and 1989-90, *op.cit.*

About 36 per cent of the credit from scheduled commercial banks goes to industry and 64 per cent to all other occupations in the State. At all India level, however, industry claims 10 per cent more. This speaks of State's relative backwardness in industry compared to other parts of the country. However, the share of transport and trade is about 11 per cent and 23 per cent against 3 per cent and 14 per cent at the all India level. Small scale industry is a favoured debtor claiming 14 per cent of the outstanding credit in India and 15.4 per cent in the State.[83]

The above data reveal that before the deterioration of law and order situation in the state, the districts of the valley had greater number of bank offices than the other two regions and the districts of Srinagar stood at 29th place in the country in total deposits. The region of Ladakh is having much lesser number of banks i.e. 22.

Industrialization

Industrialization is the most important variable of economic development. J & K is one of the industrially backward states of Indian Union. Deficiency of electricity and other sources of energy, lack of a well developed transport system, shortage of raw materials especially of minerals and political uncertainty have held up progress of industry in the State.

The J & K Industries Ltd., J & K Minerals Ltd. and J & K Handicraft Corporation that manage over thirty public sector industrial units are the chief public sector limits. The J & K Industries has a total of 17 production units which produced goods worth Rs.1307 lakhs in 1980-90 as against Rs. 2,229 lakhs during the previous year. The units employed 3,683 workers. The J & K Minerals manages Coal Mines (Kala Kote, Moghulla and Metka) gypsum mines, one cement factory (Khrew) and two precast concrete factories.[84]

The Kashmir handicrafts are known and in demand world over. They earn handsome foreign exchange and provided employment to about 2.10 lakh workers in 1989-90. The industry output suffered a loss due to disturbed situation in Kashmir from 154 crores of rupees in 1988-89 to 150 crores in 1989-90. Handloom industry is also spread over the state and engages large number of people. A corporation has been set up which implements seven development projects at Samba, Pampore, Bandipore, Udhampur, Bhaderwah, Rajauri and Leh. The Corporation also runs Kanishwal Project Kanihama, Handloom Silk Weaving Factory Rambagh, and Handloom Weaving Factory Shirinbagh. A Hill Area Development Project in Anantnag and Kupwara districts is also on the anvil. The industry provided employment to about 6000 workers and produced about 2.30 million meters of handloom cloth worth Rs. 7.16 crores. Sericulture is yet another industry that engages about 33,000 families in rearing of worms. Thousands of workers earn their living in processes of rearing, weaving, marketing and export of silk goods.[85]

If we take the percentage data (1984-85) about the total number of small scale industries registered under DICs as shown in Table No. 3.21, out of total 16,654 (100 per cent) small scale industrial units, the six districts of Kashmir had registered 53.08 per cent against 44.22 per cent in Jammu region and 2.70 per cent in Ladakh. This reveals that so far as the number of small scale industries are concerned there is no sense of relative deprivation among Kashmiris as they are in a leading position in the state but in regard to heavy industries, it is Jammu region that has an edge.

The Baribrahaman Industrial Complex in Jammu is the biggest industrial estate in the state. There are several other big and small industries in this region. In the valley there are mostly small industries of sericulture, woollen and raw silk, handicraft and tourism.[86] There are also two public-sector factories — assembly units of the HMT and ITI investment of Rs. 5 crore and 50 lakhs respectively. An industrial area for large and medium horticulture based industries has also been set up. The area will provide facilities to small scale units for fruit processing. Another industrial complex has come up at Khanmuh and a 6 million export oriented joinery mill by a local entrepreneur has also gone into production. A 600 tonnes a day capacity cement plant, a 65 million spun silk project and an electronics complex at Rangreth in Srinagar have also come up.[87] However, in respect of industry, the recent

Table No. 3.21

Small Scale Industrial Units Registered with DICs in J & K State

District	Total No. of Units	1984-85, (%)
Anantnag Pulwama	2431	(14.60)
Srinagar Budgam	4067	(24.42)
Baramulla Kupwara	2342	(14.06)
Leh	**450**	**(2.70)**
Kargil	**--**	**–**
Jammu	2706	(16.25)
Udhampur	1424	(8.55)
Rajauri	489	(2.94)
Doda	605	(3.64)
Poonch	549	(3.30)
Kathua	1591	(9.54)
J & K State	16,654 (100)	

Source : **Economic Review of J & K, 1984,** Govt. of J & K Directorate of Economics & Statistics, Planning and Development, 1985, p.44.

reports present a grim picture of the state. According to S.M.A. Qasmi, about 25 percent of small scale industries stood closed by 1992. Due to disturbed situation in the State in the last decade, about 60 to 70 percent units have been undergoing financial crisis. Out of total registered industrial units of 18,000 only 2000 units are functioning and most of these are in Jammu and Kathua districts. To rescue the small industries of financial crisis and depression the " Delayed Payment Act" is not effective in the state for its enjoying special status under Article 370. A bill for its implementation has been sent for the approval of state law department. Even the then Finance Minister Dr. Manmohan Singh declared the state industrially backward in the budget for 1993. To promote industry he has also kept the industrialists of the state out of income tax obligations.[88] In the Eighth Five Year Plan, the outlay for industry and minerals for the state of J & K is 194 crore.[89]

Therefore, the data given reveals that the regions of Ladakh and Kashmir are industrially less developed regions. Industrialization is considered as the chief criterion of determining the economic development. In fact, industrialisation has been the chief propellant behind the development of modern nation-states of the West. Hence, a lag in this respect has a direct bearing on the socio-economic development of the Kashmir region. The region of Jammu which has witnessed a much greater thrust in this area (though due to geographical and political reasons) has provided a significant field of discrimination which feeds the sense of economic deprivation, a cause found mostly behind the demands of secession or more autonomy.

The state has a forest area of 22,605 sq. kms., comprising over 15 percent of the total geographical area, excluding vast barrenness of Ladakh. Kashmir's two main natural resources are forests and water. There has been extensive devastation, with timber being supplied to Indian railways. Apart from the widespread adverse ecological impact, a high value resource was sold at virtually a throw away price which not only did not bring any substantial monetary benefits in terms of current revenues but also eroded the potentials for future income and the state's capacity for self reliance.[90] Due to the restrictions imposed on timber exports from the state by the state governments, the export faced a great decline. In 1989-90, only 98.82 (00m3) of timber was exported against the 352.03 and 191.07 (000m3) in 1983-84 and 1986-87 respectively.[91]

Tourism

Tourism is a very important activity throughout the world. It generates socio-economic benefits and promotes international brotherhood and national integration. Tourism stimulates economic activities in remote areas and leads to the development of new growth-centres. It generates new avenues of employment and foreign exchange reserved sources of a country. In Jammu & Kashmir, tourism has special significance as it stands next to agriculture and horticulture in the state as an industry. It engages thousands of people directly in providing services to tourists such as hoteliers, house-boat owners, shikara keepers, poneymen, guides etc. The industry also generates work for transporters and workers seeking their living out of handicraft industry, orchards, vegetables and food products.

A special assistance of Rs. 22.06 crores was given during the 7th Plan with which schemes like cable car, development of Pathankot and wayside facilities were taken up. Other important schemes before the Department of Tourism include International Golf Course, electrification of important tourist places like Gulmarg, Pahalgaon and

Nagin Club etc. It is also envisaged to promote addition of 50,000 beds to the existing strength and develop new tourist spots like Sonamarg, Yusmarg, Bungus, Duksum Phase I, Wullar Lake, Ahrabal Phase I, Suru Valley, Mantalai, Batote - Surinagar Jaffar Kotli landscaping, two tourist villages on East and West of Nagin and the Salal Lake.[92]

However, the most important tourism infrastructure is peace and law. Tourism in Kashmir has been subjected to great pressures both within and outside the country. The Iran-Iraq war, the turmoil in Punjab and other such factors kept the arrivals low. The decade of eighties with average of 5 to 6 lakhs of arrivals per year, saw great strains during 1983 and 1984 when the number fell to 4.40 lakhs and 2.29 lakhs respectively due to turmoil in Punjab and assassination of Indira Gandhi, the then Prime Minister and the fallout of that incident. The subsequent years registered recovery till the number of arrivals reached the record level of 7.22 lakhs in 1987 and 1988. But in following years the number of arrivals have got diminished.[93]

Since the escalation of violence, mainly from 1989-90, valley was starved of tourists. The slump in tourism made the matters worse. According to M.Y.Khan, Managing Director of J & K Tourism Development Corporation, 57,000 tourists visited the valley in 1988 and there was a 60 per cent drop in the first six months of 1989. If the tourists do not visit the valley, the economy of the valley will be ruined.[94] The number of visitors fell considerably in the following years. In the months of October, November and December 1988, the monthly arrival of tourists was 0.62, 0.53 and 0.31 (lakhs) respectively. During the same months in 1989, a sharp decline in such arrivals is visible as the figures stood 0.54, 0.44 and 0.11 (lakhs) respectively. Similarly if we compare the monthly arrivals of tourists in the valley in the months of January, February and March of 1989 and 1990, it becomes evident that tourism industry in the valley has been suffering its worst. The tourists arrivals in these months in 1989 and 1990 were 0.22, 0.17, 0.32 and 0.03, 0.01, 0.01(lakhs) respectively.[95] However, little improvement in the arrivals of tourists from foreign countries was recorded in 1992. Upto November 1992, about 9000 foreign nationals visited the valley against about 6000 in the previous year. Against it, the visits to Jammu (Vaishno Devi Shrine, Raghunath Temple etc.) and Ladakh were not affected by the turmoil in Valley. But the numerical strength of yatris to Amarnath shrine in Kashmir has also declined.[96] Though, after the installation of Farooq government in Oct.1996, tourists arrival in valley is improving year by year. According to Government of Jammu and Kashmir about 9 million tourists visited the valley in 2012.

In the region of Ladakh also tourism has significant potential. Tourism is the important source of income for Ladakhis. However, the closing of the region for tourist traffic for about six months in a year is a big hurdle in the development of tourism industry in the region.

The state of Jammu & Kashmir has been the most privileged one if we take into consideration the per capita expenditure in the state. The Table No. 3.22 shows that the per capita expenditure based on P. (Provisional outlay) has increased three times in the course of the above stated five year plans. The per capita expenditure in the state of Jammu & Kashmir exceeds the per capita expenditure in all the other states during these plans except the small states like Himachal Pradesh and Mizoram where the per capita expenditure in the eighth Five Year Plan was slightly more if compared to the state of Jammu & Kashmir.[97] Furthermore, the total outlay for the State increased about three times in the Eighth Plan if compared to the previous one.

Table No. 3.22

Per Capita Expenditure in J&K

Five Years Plans	Total Outlay for the State in Crore	Per Capita Expenditure in Rupees
VI th (1950-85)	P. Rs. 900.00 A. Rs. 918.00	1503
VII th (1985-90)	P. Rs. 1400.00 A. Rs. 2000.00	2338
VIII th (1992-97)	P. Rs. 40000.00	5138

In the Eighth Plan the major thrust area was again the power sector, the life blood of the industrialisation. The State Government has spent nearly Rs. 1200 crores on power sector during the Eighth Plan. The other thrust areas were employment generation, industrialization, agriculture and rural development.

The per capita income of the state in 1980-81 at current price was only Rs.1496 which was less than per capita income of Rs.1564 at national level. A low per capita income even after the state being one of the leading so far as per capita expenditure is concerned shows a low SDP in the state. The state SDP has suffered adversely during the nineties due to violence in the valley. Due to non-payment of power tariff, sales tax and such other taxes the state government became poorer by about Rs. 600 crore during 1990 to 93.[98]

Table No. 3.23

S.D.P. & Per Capita Income (Base year 1980-81)

Year	SDP at constant prices (Rs.in crores)	Per Capita Income at constant prices (Rs.)
1980-81	N.A.	1496
1988-89	1277.14	1804
1999-00	15660 (At Current Prices)	13816
2007-08	29039 (At Current Prices)	17590

Source: Directorate of Statistics and Economics, J&K Government. Facts, figures and details are of the Directorate, 2009.

However, the per capita income at constant prices in the state rose to 17590 in the year 2007-08. Therefore, we can notice a twelve fold increase of per capita income since the financial year 1980-81. (See Table No. 3.23)

The trend of S D P in Jammu & Kashmir is set by the performance of agriculture the most dominant sector of the state economy. The year 1987-88 was not a good year for agriculture because of low temperature during the summer months. This, as shown in Table no. 3.23 influenced directly the SDP and per capita income of the state. The disturbed situation in Kashmir in the recent years has reduced the average working hours per day and the total number of working days in the season hitting agriculture as also other activities.

To sum up the state of Jammu & Kashmir in the last four decades has underwent enormous change in almost every aspect of life. The state was the first to promulgate huge land reforms with the help of which land was transferred to the needy. A great number of educational institutions, P & T offices, bank branches, hospitals and dispensaries and other such indicators of modernisation and economic development have flourished. More than 11,000 kms. of roads have pierced the long insurmountable mountainous regions of Kashmir and Ladakh. The state, mainly Kashmir and Ladakh regions have become popular centres of tourism, cultural and religious activities. Horticulture, tourism and handicraft industries have registered a great deal of expansion. But due to shortage of the chief infrastructural facilities i.e. power, roads and communications the state has been lagging behind in development and because of this reason it fails to evoke good response from the pan-Indian bourgeoisie. The concentration of industry mainly in the Jammu region is largely due to unrestricted faith of the people in the Indian Union as also because of geographical contiguity of the region with the plains of Punjab which facilitate the communication and transportation linkages greatly.

The region of Ladakh has its own barriers, primarily the geographical and climatic conditions which make the development a dream unrealised. There is no doubt that the state is one of the industrially backward states as there are a large number of sick units with several others already closed. However, this does not mean that the routine life of the people has remained unaffected. With the spread of education, means of communication and little industrialization there have emerged new social, political and economic forces and institutions. With the spread of modernisation and economic development the traditional feudal relations have been subdued by the modern class relations. The irreconcilability of class interests brew discontent in the economically poorer sections of the society. The failure of the state government to generate employment in accordance with the requirement has resulted in resentment among the youth.

Historically it has been observed that the region of Ladakh feels estranged on account of electricity, tourism, roads, educational institutions, industries, capital inflow and general development in all. The distinct ethno-regional character of Ladakh also lends it a sense of divergence from the other two regions. The unitary character of the state constitution and less devolution of powers to Regional Councils as also funds for general welfare constitute the prime area of grievances of Ladakhis.

Notes and References

1 John Mcgarry, "Can Federalism Help to Manage Ethnic and National Diversity?" *Federations,* Vol. 4, No. 1 , March 2004, p.3.

2 *Federations,* Vol. 3, No. 2 , May 2003, p.2.

3 Harish K. Thakur, *Alienation and Integration in Jammu and Kashmir,* Jaipur : Alekh Publishers, 2000, p. 3.

4 R.B. Jain, "Political System and Nation Building : The Indian Political Experience", in S.A.H. Haqqi, (Ed.), *Democracy, Pluralism and Nation-Building,* N.Delhi :N.B.O. Publishers, 1984, pp.34-35 and *See also* Rajni Kothari, *Politics in India,* New Delhi: Orient Longman, 1972, pp.29-33.

5 D.D. Basu, *Introduction to the Constitution of India,* N. Delhi : Prentice Hall of India, 1995, p. 49.

6 *Ibid.*

7 *Constitution of Jammu and Kashmir*

8 *Constitution of India, Article 370*

9 *Ibid.*

10 Balraj Puri, "Challenge in Kashmir", *Economic and Political Weekly,* Vol XXV, No 4, January 27, 1990,

11 *Ibid.* p. 12.

12 R.K. Bhatt, "Jammu & Kashmir", in Iqbal Narain, (Ed.), *State Politics in India,* Meerut: Meenakshi Prakashan, 1976, p.150.

13 *See* Hari Ram, *Special Status in Indian Constitution: Jammu & Kashmir,* New Delhi: Seema Publications, 1983, pp. 85-134.

14 Jagmohan, *My Frozen Turbulence in Kashmir,* New Delhi: Allied Publishers, 1991, p.220.

15 *Daily Excelsior,* October 8, 1987.

16 Harish K. Thakur, *op.cit,* p.84

17 *Ibid.,* p.85.

18 *Ibid.*

19 *Data India,* October and November, 1987.

20 *Ibid.,* November 15, 1987.

21 *Ibid.,* November 19 & 21, 1987.

22 A.Baruah , " J & K : A Sensitive Move", *Frontline,* November 28, December 11, 1987, p.19.

23 Jagmohan, *op.cit.,* pp.221-22.

24 *Ibid.,* p.222.

25 M.K.Tikku, "NC Stumbling Block to Hill Council", *The Hindustan Times,* October 5, 1992.

26 Harish K. Thakur, *op.cit.* p. 86.

27 *Ibid.,* p.87.

28 *Ibid.*

29 *Ibid.*

30 *Data India,* October 23-29, 1989, p.513.

31 Jagmohan, *op.cit.,* p.216.

32 Balraj Puri, *op.cit.,* p.14.

33 *Ibid.,* p.12.

34 Harish K. Thakur, *op.cit.* p.88.

35 Alstair Lamb, *Kashmir: A Disputed Legacy, 1946-1990*, Karachi: Oxford University Press, 1992, pp.323, 332-33.

36 Ravinder Kumar, "Anguish of Kashmiris: An Agenda for Countering Alienation" , *The Times of India*, May, 1992.

37 *Ibid*

38 *Data India*, March 16-23, 1990.

39 Achin Vinaik, " Overplaying Balkanization Dragon to India", *Indian Express*, October 5, 1992.

40 *Census of India*, 1981, Ser.8, *op.cit.*

41 Puri. *op.cit.*, 1981, p.20.

42 *Census of India*, 1981, op.cit.

43 *Ibid.*

44 http://censusindia.gov.in/2011-prov-results/prov_data_products_J&K.html

45 *Ibid.*

46 During the period 1989-90, 250 new schools were anticipated to have been opened and 8th standard added to 30 and 10th to 13 schools. *Economic Review of J & K 1990*, (Government of J & K: Directorate of Economics & Statistics Planning & Development, 1981), p.34.

47 *University Handbook*, A 14, New Delhi, Ajanta Publications, 1989, pp.643-50.

48 *Census Atlas*, op.cit., p.114,

49 *Ibid.*, pp.114-15.

50 *Economic Review of J & K, 1990*, op.cit., pp.47-48.

51 *Economic Review of J & K, 1990*, op.cit., pp.30-31.

52 *Ibid.*, p.30.

53 T.Bose, D. Mohan, G. Navlakha and S. Banerjee, "India's Kashmir War", *Economic and Political Weekly*, March 31, 1990, p.660.

54 *Ibid.*

55 *Ibid.*, p. 661.

56 *Ibid.*

57 *Ibid.*, pp.20-22, and *Indian Economic Diary*, Vol. XVII No.41, Oct. 8-14, 1986, p.10936.

58 *Ibid.*, p.21.

59 D.N. Ghosh, "Kashmir and India", *Economic and Political Weekly*, Vol. XXVI , No. 34, August 24, 1991, p.1961.

60 *Indian Economic Diary*, Vol. XXIII No. 24, June 10-16, 1992, p.13295.

61 *Ibid.*

62 *Ibid.*, Vol. XXIII, No. 29, July 15-21, 1992, p.13331.

63 *Ibid.*, p.123123, Vol. XXIII No.31, July 29 - August 4, 1991, p.13351 and Vol. XXIV No.4, Jan 22-23, 1993, p.13551.

64 http://www. http://jkspdc.nic.in/

65 *Ibid.*

66 Ghosh, *op.cit.*, p.1962.

67 *Economic Review of J & K, 1989-90*, op.cit., p.13.

68 *Ibid.*

69 *Ibid.*, p.14.

70 *Economic Review of J & K, 1990*, op.cit., pp.57-59.

71 *Irrigation Statistics : 1950-51 to 1985-86*, Government of J & K : Directorate of Economics & Statistics, Planning & Development, 1987, p.12.

72 Government of J & K : Directorate of Economics & Statistics, Planning & Development, 1987, p.12. and *Digest of Statistics 2001-02*, Government of J & K : Directorate of Economics & Statistics, Planning & Development, 2003, p. 100.

73 *Economic Review of J & K 1990,* op.cit., pp.57-59

74 *Ibid.,* p.15

75 *Indian Express,* March 31, 1993.

76 *Ibid.*

77 M.K.Tikku, "Kashmir Today III, Economy remains Unaffected ", *The Hindustan Times,* October 2, 1992.

78 *Socio-Economic Profile of Jammu and Kashmir-2009,* Directorate of Economics and Statistics, 2009, Jammu and Kashmir, 2010, pp. 185-231.

79 *Economic Review of J & K, 1989-90,* op.cit., p. XXIV.

80 *Indicators of Regional Development : 1985-86,* op.cit., p.17

81 *Performance Review of Jammu and Kashmir 2008-09,* Directorate of Economics and Statistics, Jammu and Kashmir, p.121.

82 *Economic Review of J & K 1990,* op.cit., p.27.

83 *Ibid.,* pp.27-28.

84 *Ibid.,* pp.24-25.

85 *Ibid.,* p.26.

86 *Sri Directory of Industries of India,* Delhi : Small Industries Research Institute, Chapter 16, p.2.

87 *The Times of India Directory & Year Book 1984,* Bombay : The Times of India Press, 1985, p.27.

88 Harish K. Thakur, op.cit., p.114.

89 *Eighth Five Year Plan 1992-97,* Vol. II, Government of India, Planning Commission, N. Delhi.

90 D.N.Ghosh, *op.cit.,* p.1959.

91 *Economic Review of J & K, 1990,* op.cit., p.70.

92 *Economic Review of J & K 1990,* op.cit., p.32.

93 *Ibid.* p.33.

94 Harish K. Thakur, *op.cit.,* p.92.

95 *Jammu and Kashmir in Indian Economy,* Directorate of Economics & Statistics, Planning & Development Department, 1990, p.19.

96 *Ibid.,* p.20.

97 *Eighth Five Year Plan,* Vol.II, Government of India, Planning Commission, pp.215, 126. During the 6th & 7th Five Year Plans, per capita expenditure was determined as per 1981 Census whereas that of 8th Five Year Plan the determining figures are the projected population of the state by the Standing Committee of Experts on Population projections. According to the Committee in its report of October 1989, the population of the state was about 77.19 lakhs.

98 *Indian Economic Diary,* Vol. XXIV, No.9, Feb. 26-March 4,1993, p.13593

Chapter 4

Inter-Regional Divergence and Ladakh -I

(Social, Economic and Cultural)

Theoretically the concepts of society, economy and polity may appear to be three independent entities but they don't operate separately rather they derive from each other and sustain on the principles of mutuality and interdependence. While society signifies the web of relations and social structure in which they evolve the economy broadly encapsulates the evolution of market and class structure which in a way tend to undermine the former in its march towards progress. Polity though might have myriad of shapes and kinds in a given society, its sustenance largely depends on the interplay of socio-economic forces in the society.

If social factors like race, language, religion, culture *et.al.* play a significant role in the formation of an ethnicity or nationality, the economic factors can also play havoc with the social web. The role of language, race, religion and culture has been crucial in contemporary times in the determination of political status of people. The examples of Quebec Province in Canada, Belgium, South Africa, Bangladesh, Pakistan, North Ireland, Germany, India and many more establish the inexorable role of ethnicity and culture in the determination of political standings of the people. The example of Jammu and Kashmir is one of its kind in India and what if the theory extends to its region of Ladakh and Jammu within the state.

The current chapter focuses primarily on the socio-economic factors which provide Ladakhis a sense of separate selfhood, an identity, a commonality that inspires the people of the region that they deserve to be treated as a separate political unit. It is in the backdrop of these factors that the demands of political nature i.e. political status, structure, process of interest articulation and aspirations of people can be duly analysed.

During the study we have adopted different tools and techniques for the analysis and interpretation of the data. SPSS is generally meant to analyse large data but we have resorted to it for comparatively a small sample of 200 respondents. The major among them are $\overline{X}$, Standard Deviation, P. Value, Kurtosis, Skewness and Chi Square. This chapter hightlights the socio-economic status of the people of Ladakh vis-á-vis the people of Jammu and Kashmir. The purpose of the study is also to delineate the impact of the process of globalization and modernizing wheels over the social, cultural, religious and economic life of the people of Ladakh.

The people of Ladakh have an obvious cultural and communal dissimilarity with the other two regions of the state i.e. Jammu and Kashmir. It is but imminent to get the Ladakhi opinion over the fact and as the Table No. 4.1 shows Ladakhis verify the statement.

Table 4.1

Variable 1	1 SD	2 D	3 PA	4 A	5 SA	$\overline{X}$	St. Dev	Skew	Kurt	X^2	P. Value
People of Ladakh are different from the people of other two regions: Jammu and Kashmir			12	24	164	4.76	.555	-2.285	-4.299	53.56	<0.05

Source: Field Survey, data collected through interview schedules circulated among respondents.

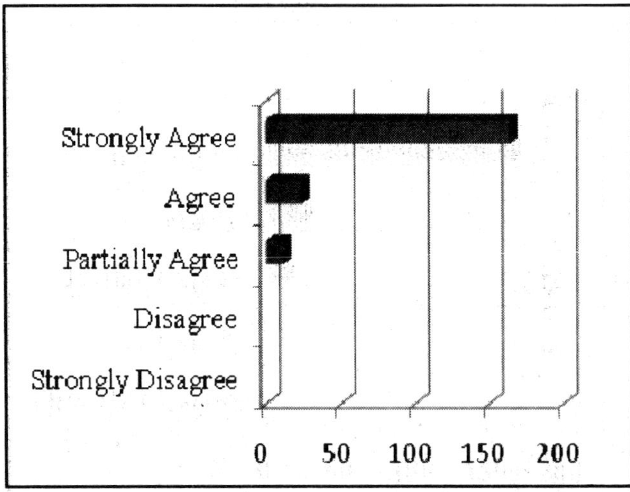

Fig 4.1 Cultural and Communal Dissimilarity among the Regions

It is evident about the respondent's opinion regarding the variable 'People of Ladakh are different from the people of Jammu & Kashmir' that the mean value of the opinion is more than the standard average i.e. three at five point scale. The variation in the opinion is .555 and skewness is recorded at -2.285 which reveals that the data is more scattered towards higher side. While applying X^2 test of goodness at fit it rejects the null hypothesis at 5% level of significance. It shows that the distribution of opinion is unequal. Thus the above analysis leads us to conclude that the respondents agree with the fact that the people of Ladakh are different from the people of Jammu & Kashmir on account of their separate identity based on language, culture, religion and society.

Evolved over millenniums, the people of Ladakh have distinct social and cultural values of their own. The wheels of development and progress i.e. modernization definitely work on this dimension of life of a people. Table No. 4.2 ascertains the view of Ladakhis over this.

Table 4.2

Variable 2	1 SD	2 D	3 PA	4 A	5 SA	$\overline{X}$	St. Dev	Skew	Kurt	X^2	P. Value
The social and cultural life of the people of Ladakh is flourishing as normal	4	32	24	104	36	3.68	1.019	-.754	-.108	53.56	<0.05

Source: Field Survey, data collected through interview schedules circulated among respondents.

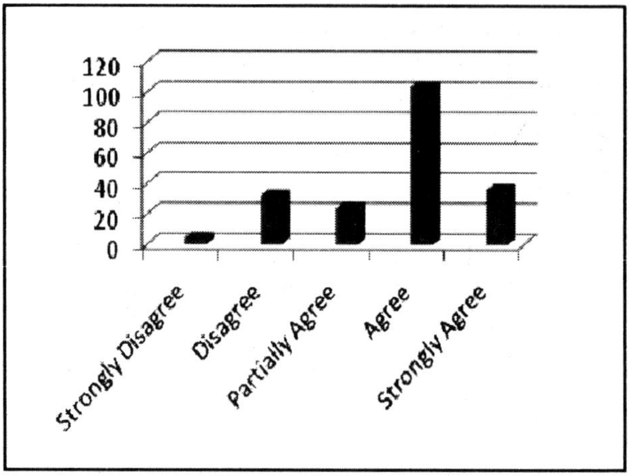

It is manifest about the respondent's opinion regarding the variable 'The social and cultural life of the people of Ladakh is flourishing as normal' that the mean value of the opinion is more than the standard average i.e. three at five point scale. The variation in the opinion is 1.019 and skewness is recorded at -.754 with -.108 Kurtosis. This reveals that the data is more scattered towards higher side. While applying X^2 test of goodness at fit it rejects the null hypothesis at 5% level of significance. It manifests that the distribution of opinion is unequal. Thus the above analysis leads us to conclude that the respondents largely agree with the fact that the social and cultural life of the people of Ladakh is flourishing as normal. However, in the ensuing questions they also cast aspersions over the fact and believe that the process of globalization (role of media, advent of market, IT revolution, communications and development) has endangered the cultural fabric of the region.

Ladakhis are also of the view that people here sincerely stick to their culture, traditions and values. The Table No. 4.3 corresponds to the said variable.

Table 4.3

Variable 3	1 SD	2 D	3 PA	4 A	5 SA	$\overline{X}$	St. Dev	Skew	Kurt	X^2	P. Value
People adhere to their culture, traditions, values and festivals as always	–	–	16	76	108	4.46	.645	-.794	-.361	16.3	<0.05

Source: Field Survey, data collected through interview schedules circulated among respondents.

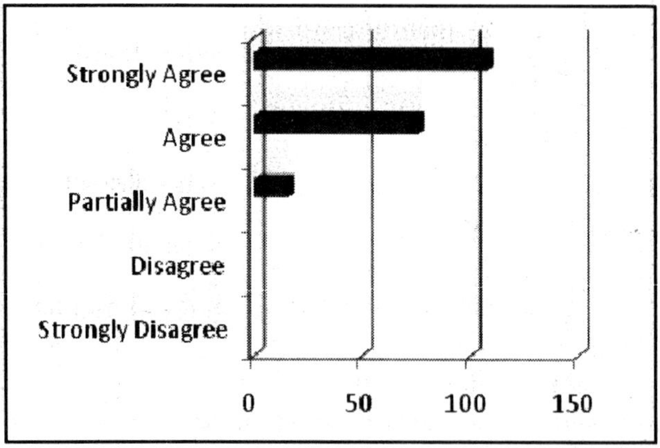

Regarding the variable 'People adhere to their culture, traditions, values and festivals as always' it has been observed that the mean value of the opinion (4.46) is more than the standard average i.e. three at five point scale. The variation in the opinion is .645 and skewness is recorded at -.794 which reveals that the data is more scattered towards higher side. The use of X^2 test of goodness at fit rejects the null hypothesis at 5% level of significance. It shows that the distribution of opinion is unequal.Thus the above analysis leads us to conclude that the respondents agree with the fact that the People adhere to their culture, traditions, values and festivals as always and not much shift has been noticed in this arena of life. This is noteworthy that in the changed global scenario Ladakhis still cherish their customs and cultural values.

However, the following analysis (Table No. 4.4) records that the younger generation tends to deviate from their traditions and culture.

Table 4.4

Variable 4	1 SD	2 D	3 PA	4 A	5 SA	$\overline{X}$	St. Dev	Skew	Kurt	X^2	P. Value
The youth (15 yrs. to 40 yrs.) of the region is indifferent towards traditional values and ways of life	–	40	88	64	08	3.20	.808	-.097	-.579	17.5	<0.05

Source: Field Survey, data collected through interview schedules circulated among respondents.

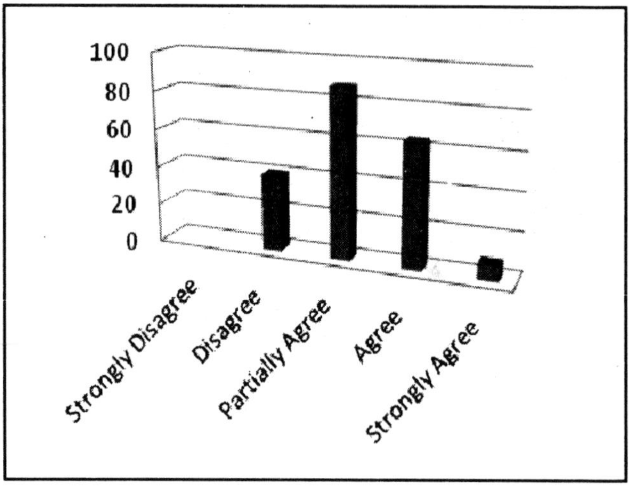

It is observed about the indifference of the youth towards their traditional values and ways of life that the mean value (3.20) of the opinion is more than the standard average i.e. three at five point scale. The variation in the opinion is .808 and skewness is recorded at .097 which reveals that the data is more scattered towards higher side. While applying X^2 test of goodness at fit it rejects the null hypothesis at 5% level of significance. It shows that the distribution of opinion is unequal. Thus the above analysis leads us to conclude that the respondents broadly agree with the fact that the youth (15 yrs. to 40 yrs.) of the region is indifferent towards traditional values and ways of life and shows less interest in their culture, traditions, customs etc. Of course the impact of consumer culture and media unleashed by the forces of globalization can be observed over the minds of younger people who are more literate and exposed to the world than the older one.

Table 4.5

Variable 5	1 SD	2 D	3 PA	4 A	5 SA	$\overline{X}$	St. Dev	Skew	Kurt	X^2	P. Value
Has the social structure (social hierarchy traditions and customs changed)	–	48	88	32	32	3.24	1.001	-507	-.717	10.4	<0.05

Source: Field Survey, data collected through interview schedules circulated among respondents.

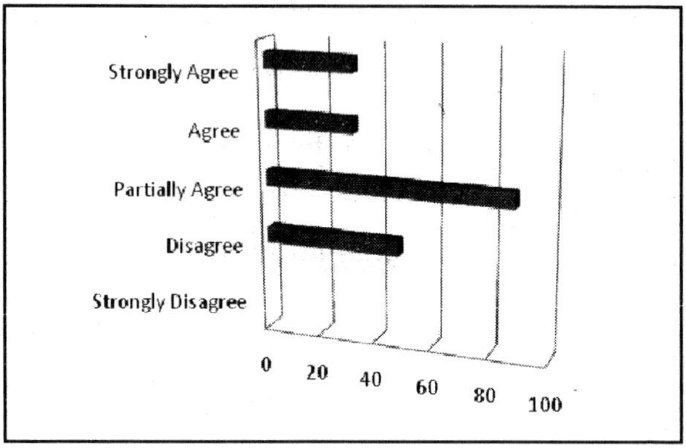

The fear of loss of identity, cultural values and traditions further aggravates as majority of the respondents again believe that the social structure of the region is undergoing change. This however, goes contrary to the previous opinion expressed by respondents that people still adhere to their cultural values as a good number of them believe that 'yes' the cultural fabric of the region is gradually weakening and giving way to the forces of globalization.

Regarding the view that the social structure (social hierarchy, customs and traditions) have changed it has been observed that mean value (3.24) of the opinion is more than the standard average i.e. three at the five point scale. The variation in the opinion is 1.001 and skewness is recorded at -.507 that shows the scattering of the data towards higher side. . While applying X^2 test of goodness at fit it rejects the null hypothesis at 5% level of significance. It shows that the distribution of opinion is unequal. Thus the above analysis leads us to conclude that the respondents are broadly divided over the view but a slight majority of them approve of the view that the social structure (social hierarchy, traditions and customs) have changed over the years.

Table 4.6

Variable No 6	1 SD	2 D	3 PA	4 A	5 SA	$\overline{X}$	St. Dev	Skew	Kurt	X^2	P·Value
The process globalization (increased literacy, connectivity, development and modermization) has influenced the social and cultural relations and festivals of the people of Ladakh	–	24	56	48	72	3.84	1.056	-.316	-1.189	6.00	<0.05

Source : Field Survey, data collected through interview schedules circulated among respondents.

The process of globalization that permeates to the remotest of the corners of world has influenced the society, culture and values of Ladakh also. Today people are more accustomed to the luxuries that technology has offered and global market has reached at their door. With the rapid growth of literacy in the region people have become more conscious of the available opportunities in material and services. This changes the primordial assumptions and values of a society as people tend to look for the better ways of life. This seems to be true about the people of Ladakh also as the following variable confirms this.

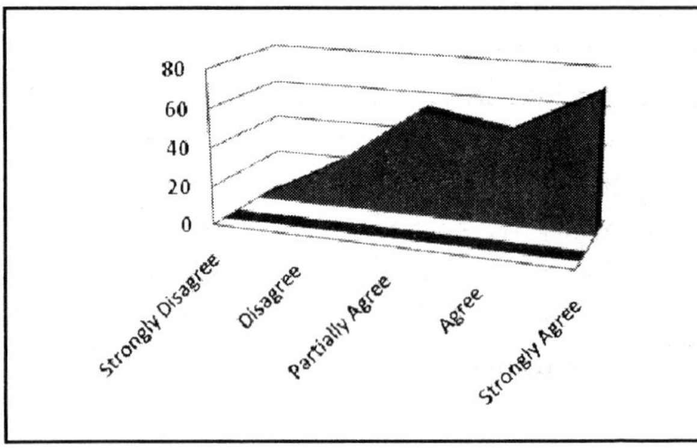

It is evident about the respondent's opinion regarding the variable "the process of globalization (increased connectivity, development and modernization) has influenced the social and cultural relations and festivals of the people of Ladakh" that the mean value of the opinion is more than the standard average i.e. three at five point scale. The variation in the opinion is 1.056 and skewness is recorded at -.316 which reveals that the data is more scattered towards higher side. While applying X^2 test of goodness at fit it rejects the null hypothesis at 5% level of significance. It shows that the distribution of opinion is unequal. Thus the above analysis leads us to conclude that the respondents agree with the fact that the process of globalization has left deep impact on the socio-cultural life of the people of Ladakh.

The flow of technology and the advent of modernizing forces like transport, communications and services that in turn facilitate the inflow of market forces, industry, and tourism etc. and upgrade the living standards of people also affect the geo-spatiality and ecology of a region. We have witnessed this in India and around that global warming has caused melting of high mountains and glaciers in Himachal Pradesh, Jammu and Kashmir, Uttaranchal and Arunachal Pradesh. This causes severe ecological and natural disasters to a region. The unexpected cloud burst and floods of Leh in August 2010 that destroyed property worth millions and took several lives might be one of the outcomes of this kind of development. The people of Ladakh feel highly scared of the phenomenon since it is first of its kind in the region for centuries and blame the undue construction, increased vehicular traffic and forestation by Indian forces as the cause behind it.

Table 4.7

Variable No 7	1 SD	2 D	3 PA	4 A	5 SA	$\overline{X}$	St. Dev	Skew	Kurt	X^2	P·Value
The process of modernization and globalization has left great impact on the environment of the region of Ladakh	–	–	28	116	56	4.14	.639	-.126	-.499	15.1	<0.05

Source : Field Survey, data collected through interview schedules circulated among respondents

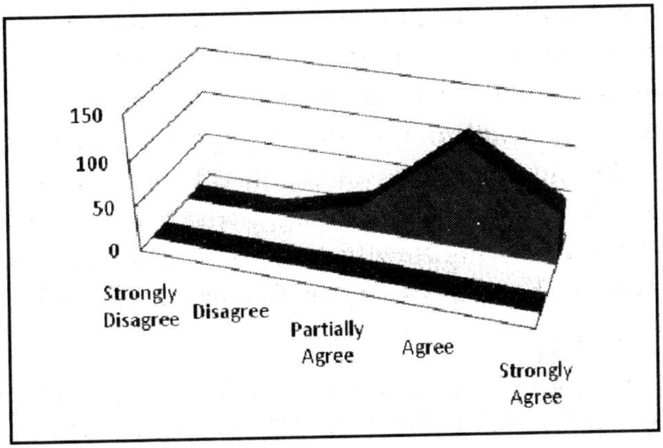

From the Variable No. 7 'the process of modernization and globalization has left great impact on the environment of the region of Ladakh', it has been observed that mean value (4.14) of the opinion is more than the standard average i.e. three at the five point scale. The variation in the opinion is .639 and skewness is recorded at -.126 that shows the scattering of the data towards higher side. . While applying X^2 test of goodness at fit it rejects the null hypothesis at 5% level of significance. It shows that the distribution of opinion is unequal. Thus the above analysis leads us to conclude that the respondents agree with the fact that the process of modernization and globalization has left great impact on the environment of the region of Ladakh.

Globalization has been received as a process that has added to the existing division and rifts in people. With the breakup of the stringent state regimentations and the free flow of goods, capital, investment, technology and the world's becoming a battleground of the competing trans-national groups and multi-nationals the ideas of protectionism and welfare have suffered adversely against the gigantism of market. In the current surge of events if the states are to witness immense increase in production and income the marginalized ones are to get further alienated and this is a matter of grave concern for the protagonists of the poor and the marginalized. It has been observed that not only in the developing world but even in the developed states the peripheralisation of socially and economically poor people is taking place. The demands for the ouster of foreigners in U.S. and U.K. are just a symptomatical manifestation of the phenomenon having deeper roots.

Development has its negatives too. If on the one hand it leads to general uplift in life standards of people it is also causative of interest consciousness and consequently conflicts. Development in a particular region can be a cause of concern for relatively less developed regions, a phenomenon true of Jammu and Kashmir. The regions of Jammu and Ladakh have been raising the issue of discrimination by Valley over the decades. As discussed in the previous chapter the region of Ladakh feels deprived in the fields of educational institutions, health institutions, roads, tourism and many other areas. This is established by the respondents in the ensuing variable.

Table 4.8

Variable No 8	1 SD	2 D	3 PA	4 A	5 SA	$\overline{X}$	St. Dev	Skew	Kurt	X^2	P.Value
The process of globalization/ modernization has added to the fissures among different regions of the state	–	56	72	60	12	3.14	.903	.232	-.849	10.3	<0.05

Source: Field Survey, data collected through interview schedules circulated among respondents.

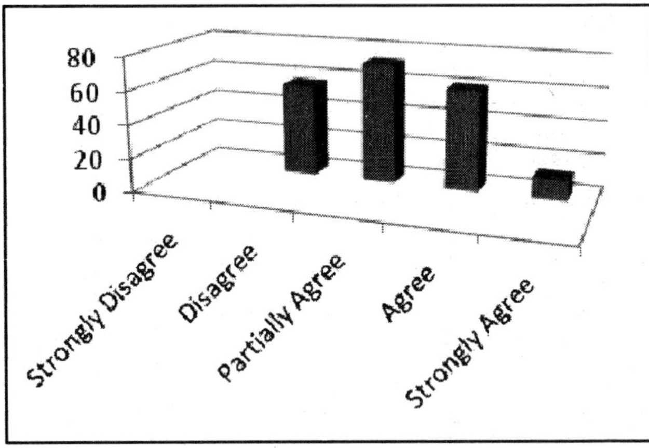

It has been observed about the view 'the process of globalization/modernization has added to the fissures among different regions of the state' that the mean value (3.14) of the opinion is higher than the standard average i.e. three at the five point scale. The variation in the opinion is .903 and skewness is recorded at -.232 that shows the scattering of the data towards higher side. While applying X^2 test of goodness of fit the null hypothesis at 5% level of significance is rejected. It shows that the distribution of opinion is unequal. Although, the opinion is largely scattered between agreement and disagreement with a majority of them showing neutrality yet the above analysis leads us to conclude that the respondents are of the view that the process of globalization/modernization has added to the fissures among different regions i.e. Jammu, Kashmir and Ladakh of the state. Of course the reference is towards the development and governance side where the regions of Ladakh and Jammu feel estranged because of neglect.

Closely associated is the question of cultural identity of the people. The Ladakhis, as is true of most of the tribes in India, feel that the modernizing and globalizing forces are weakening the cultural fabric and old customs and traditions in favour of consumerism and luxuries of time.

Table 4.9

Variable No 9	1 Y	2 N	$\overline{X}$	St. Dev	Skew	Kurt	X^2	P. Value
The process globalization modernization has endangered the separate identity of the people of Ladakh	164	36	1.18	.388	1.718	-.989	20.4	<0.05

Source : Field Survey, data collected through interview schedules circulated among respondents.

From the Table 4.9 in response to variable 'the process of globalization/modernization has endangered the separate identity of the people of Ladakh' it has been observed that the mean value (1.18) of the opinion is higher than the standard average i.e. 1.5 at the two point scale. The variation in the opinion is .388 and skewness is recorded at 1.718 that shows the scattering of the data towards higher side. While applying X^2 test of goodness of fit the null hypothesis at 5% level of significance is rejected. It shows that the distribution of opinion is unequal. The above analysis makes it crystal clear that Ladakhis strongly affirm that the process of globalization/modernization has endangered the separate identity of the people of Ladakh. About 82 % respondents agree with the fact that the separate cultural identity of Ladakh is in danger and requires to be protected.

Economically the region of Ladakh has registered a considerable growth in literacy in the last two decades. There has been a significant development in roads, transport, communications and tourism (See Chapter 3). The economy of the region has registered a noteworthy growth. The current section deals with the primary facilities of education, health, roads etc, in the region of Ladakh at economic level.

Schools are reflective of the level of education in a particular region. The number of schools and the area they feed speak of the general development of a society. The region of Ladakh enjoys the facility of sufficient number of schools.

Table 4.10

Variable N.10	1 Y	2 N	$\overline{X}$	St. Dev	Skew	Kurt	X^2	P. Value
Is there a school in your area?	200	nil	1.00	.00	–	–	–	–

Source : Field Survey, data collected through interview schedules circulated among respondents.

Education is the paramount criterion of development of a region. The multifaceted development of the personality of an individual derives primarily from this factor. More a people are literate more the region developed. It is evident about the respondent's opinion regarding the variable 'Is there a school in your area' that the facility of school is available in almost whole of the region. All the respondents replied in positive yes about the availability of schools in the region. It seems to be a hard earned applause on behalf of the government of Jammu & Kashmir to provide the facility in a region that is sparsely populated amid horrid terrains.

Table 4.11

Variable No. 11	1 Y	2 N	$\bar{X}$	St. Dev	Skew	Kurt	X^2	P. Value
Are there sufficient teachers in your school?	176	24	1.00	.00	–	–	–	–

Source : Field Survey, data collected through interview schedules circulated among respondents.

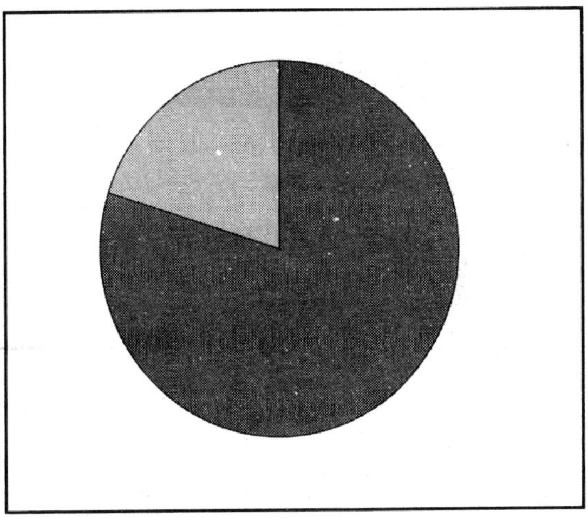

Asked about the availability of sufficient staff in the schools vide variable 'Are there sufficient teachers in your school' the respondent's opinion has been registered in affirmative 'yes'. Although about 12% of the respondents disapprove with the idea, yet the good majority of the respondents does not have much problems with the availability of teachers in the schools thus providing a sigh of relief to the ruling government.

Table 4.12

Variable No. 12	1 Y	2 N	$\overline{X}$	St. Dev	Skew	Kurt	X^2	P. Value
Is there any college in your area?	160	40	1.20	.404	1.547	0407	18.0	<0.05

Source : Field Survey, data collected through interview schedules circulated among respondents.

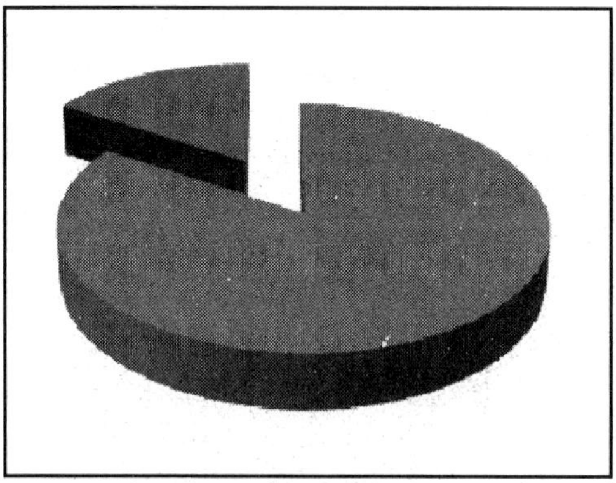

Higher education imparted through colleges is a significant development catalyst agent of an area that reveals about the socio-economic and political evolution of a people. About the availability of colleges in the region vide variable 'Is there any college in your area' the respondent's opinion has again been registered in affirmative 'yes'. Although about 20% of the respondents disagree over the presence of a college in their area yet the good majority of the respondents (80%) has approved that they are having a college in their area. As per data available there are only two degree colleges (one each in Kargil and Leh) and few polytechnic colleges in the region and since the region is sparsely populated the colleges seem to be at far reaching ends to the peripheral people. The widely scattered populace over the area may have ambition for colleges but the geographical barriers and the lack of student feedback make such possibilities feeble. Health is another factor with the help of which the development index of a region can be evaluated. The availability of health institutions such as primary health centres, hospitals and dispensaries speak of the collective consciousness of a people towards better life as also the life

Table 4.13

Variable No. 13	1 Y	2 N	$\overline{X}$	St. Dev	Skew	Kurt	X^2	P. Value
Do you have any hospital in the area?	168	32	1.16	.370	1.913	1.726	23.1	<0.05

Source : Field Survey, data collected through interview schedules circulated among respondents.

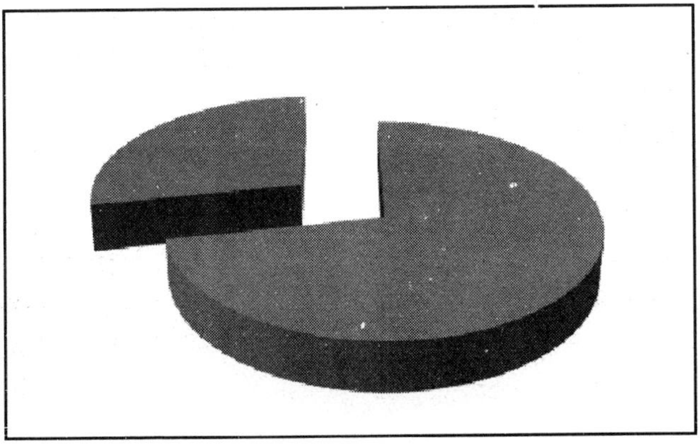

expectancy and longevity of a people. Only a healthy people can be interest conscious and seekers of their just rights in a system. It is evident from the respondent's opinion regarding the variable 'Do you have any hospital in the area' that the facility of hospitals is mostly available in the region. A good majority of the respondents (84%) replied in positive 'yes' about the availability of hospitals in their region. About 16% of the respondents disapprove with the fact that they are having hospitals in their areas.

So far as the availability of this basic amenity is concerned, the state government is advised to meet up the said requirement, since, if people have to move to long distances for getting medical aid then it counts to be its denial. In many such cases people show reluctance in taking their patients to hospitals and even don't go for timely health care, thus resulting in health hazards. Taken into account the hardships of the region it is also advisable that small movable Medi Centres with a doctor and requisite staff together with well equipped labs can also be resorted to.

Table 4.14

Variable No. 14	1 Y	2 N	$\overline{X}$	St. Dev	Skew	Kurt	X^2	P. Value
Are doctors always available in the hospitals?	144	56	1.28	.453	1.011	-1.021	9.68	<0.05

Source : Field Survey, data collected through interview schedules circulated among respondents

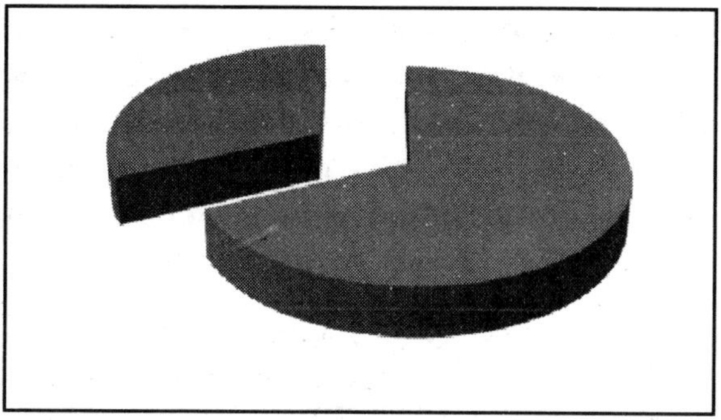

The situation appears worse when asked about the availability of sufficient staff (doctors and nurses) in the hospitals through the question 'Are doctors always available in the hospitals'. About 72% respondents are of the opinion that doctors are available in the hospitals. However, 28% of the respondents negate the affirmation which reveals the discontent of the people ıegarding the non-availability of doctors and hospitals. It leaves a big task for the government to be performed in due course of time.

Table 4.15

Variable No. 15	1 Y	2 N	$\overline{X}$	St. Dev	Skew	Kurt	X^2	P. Value
Do you get free medicines easily at the hospital?	136	64	1.32	.471	.796	-1.425	23.1	<0.05

Source: Field Survey, data collected through interview schedules circulated, among respondents.

Asked about the availability of free medicines in the hospitals through the variable 'Do you get free medicines easily at the hospitals' the percentage of the respondents further dips to 68 %. About 32 % of the respondents disapprove with the statement that adds to the degree of discontentment of the people regarding the non-availability of doctors, hospitals and free medicines.

Therefore, the state government is advised to go for disposing of the abovementioned facilities to the people of Ladakh in the coming times so that the discontent prevalent regarding the non-availability of medicines and doctors could be attenuated.

Table 4.16

Variable No. 16	1 Y	2 N	$\overline{X}$	St. Dev	Skew	Kurt	X^2	P. Value
Is your village/town connected with road?	128	72	1.36	.484	.602	-1.708	3.92	<0.05

Source : Field Survey, data collected through interview schedules circulated among respondents.

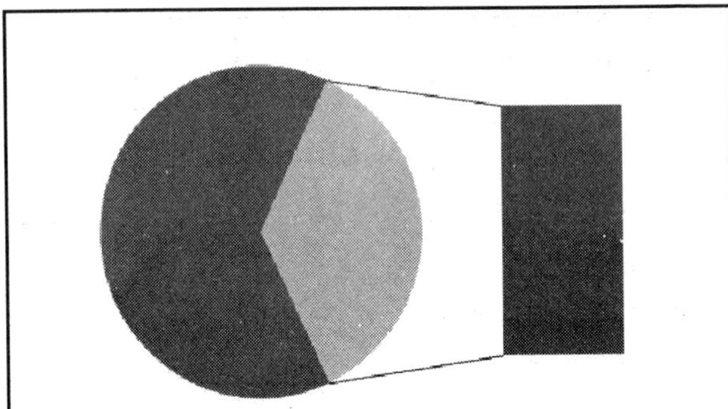

Roads constitute the veins of a region since without them no development is feasible. It is through roads only that an area registers multidimensional development. They are not only helpful in import and export of essential commodities but also in making human life more secure and meaningful. They are one of the prime means of evaluation of the development index of a region. More a state or area has road network more developed it is considered.

If we take into account the variable "Is your village/ town connected with road" about 64% of the respondents affirmed the statement that they are connected with roads. However, a big chunk of 36% respondents denied the availability of road facility. This factor can be one of the significant reasons behind the development of the sense of regional divergence in Ladakh area. If the region is left behind in road network more are the chances of development lag. Even the per capita income of an area also largely depends on the road network because they constitute the real base of the economic and commercial activities of an area. The Manali-Leh and Srinagar-Kargil-Leh national highways are maintained by the Ministry of Defence. The state government is only left with the task of development of intra-regional roads. Although, the geographical limitations and the huge investment that roads incur seem to be the chief barrier in the spread of road network. Still the state government is advised to increase the amount of budgetary head of road expenditure in the region. More the people are connected by roads more the sense of legitimacy of governance prevails.

Table 4.17

Variable No. 17	1 Y	2 N	$\bar{X}$	St. Dev	Skew	Kurt	X^2	P. Value
If yes are they metalled?	84	116	1.58	.498	-.334	-1.969	1.28	<0.05

Source : Field Survey, data collected through interview schedules circulated among respondents.

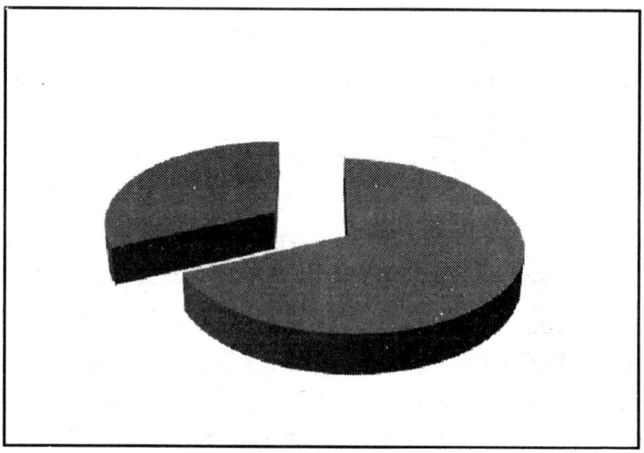

Good metalled roads ensure safer and smooth transportation. The situation worsens over the length of metalled roads. Asked "Whether the roads are metalled" 53% of the respondents replied that the roads are not metalled. In such a sensitive area that borders with Pakistan and China the quality of roads has to be the best and road network vast. China has laid railway line up to Lhasa with huge road network and airstrips in Tibet. This poses a serious strategic threat to India since China lays claim to a vast territory around this region also. Here it becomes essential for the Union Government too to go for a serious evaluation of the situation and expand the budgetary flow towards this direction too.

Table 4.18

Variable No. 18	1 Y	2 N	$\overline{X}$	St. Dev	Skew	Kurt	X^2	P. Value
Do you have post office in your area?	144	56	1.28	.453	1.011	-1.021	9.68	<0.05

Source : Field Survey, data collected through interview schedules circulated among respondents.

Postal and communication services constitute another important element over which the development of a region greatly relies. It is through these services that a well coordinated effort towards development takes place. Poorer the services lesser would be the efficiency in work. Asked about "Do you have post office in your area" 72% respondents replied in affirmative 'yes' while 28% denied the availability of postal facility. As the Table no 4.18 shows the data is skewed towards higher side at 1.011 with kurtosis at -1.021. Yet a significant portion is left without the facility thus leaving a good deal of job to be done by government.

Table 4.19

Variable No. 19	1 Y	2 N	$\bar{X}$	St. Dev	Skew	Kurt	X^2	P. Value
Do you have small market in your village/ town?	144	56	1.28	.453	1.011	-1.021	9.68	<0.05

Source : Field Survey, data collected through interview schedules circulated among respondents.

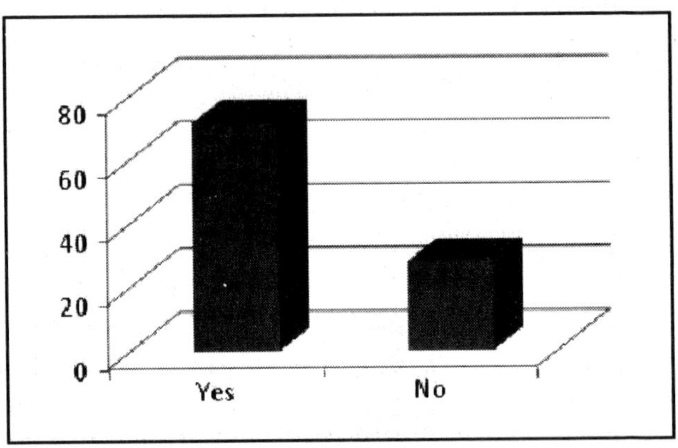

Market is reflective of the general living standards of people as also the commerce and trade related activities of an area. It also signifies the purchase value of a people which in turn reflects the income. Asked about the availability of market in their areas 72% respondents expressed that they had markets in their villages or towns. Only 28%

respondents denied the fact that market was there in their areas. However, market is not something which is feasible and easily available at village level and even an access of 5 kms. to 10 kms. of a market is also considered convenient. Even the market that is available in villages, as experienced by researcher, is just of supplementary kind that covers the routine sundry goods and local products.

Table 4.20

Variable No. 20	1 Y	2 N	$\bar{X}$	St. Dev	Skew	Kurt	X^2	P. Value
Do you have sufficient water supply?	152	48	1.24	.431	1.256	-.443	13.5	<0.05

Source : Field Survey, data collected through interview schedules circulated among respondents.

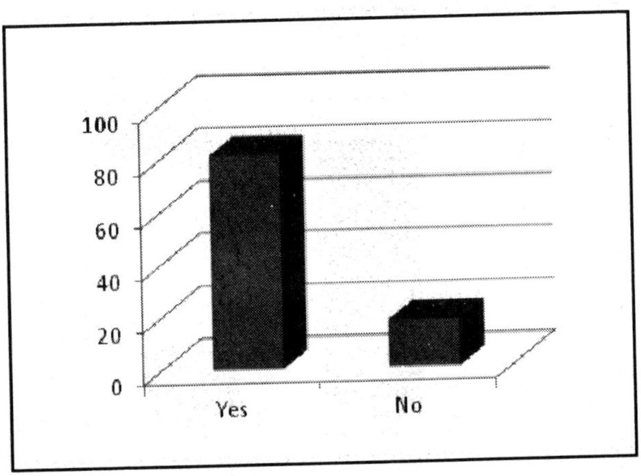

Drinkable water is an important signifier of development. Though the region of Leh is having abundance of natural water resources yet its supply to the villages and towns is a factor worth analysing. About 76% respondents accept that they are having sufficient water supply in their areas. 24% respondents, however, express disappointment over the supply of water. This seems to be yet another area of grievance where state government has to take adequate steps.

Table 4.21

Variable No. 21	1 Y	2 N	$\overline{X}$	St. Dev	Skew	Kurt	X^2	P. Value
Is your village/ town totally electrified?	164	36	1.18	.388	1.718	.989	20.48	<0.05

Source : Field Survey, data collected through interview schedules circulated among respondents.

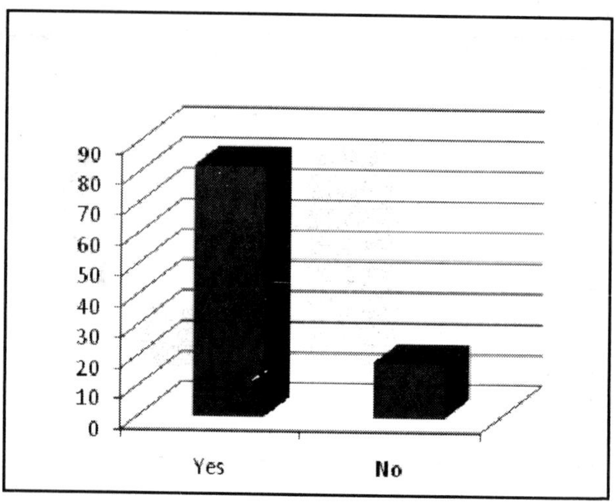

Today electricity is the prime element that boosts the engine of life. It is electricity that is basic to industries, household work, institutions and offices. An area becomes crippled without it and even a thought of its absence would be a nightmare in 21st century. Asked about the availability of electricity in their villages or towns, 82% respondents approved that they had this facility. It is sad to know that still 18% of the respondents are bereft of this facility. In a region which remains cut off from the rest of the world for about 7 to 8 months because of inclement and harsh weather and where temperature hovers around -30⁰C to-10⁰C the importance of electricity can well be imagined. Jammu and Kashmir is a state with huge potential for the production of hydro-electric power and the city of Leh and Kargil are situated on the banks of Sindhu and Suru rivers. It is not unlikely to go for such power projects which at least meet the requirements of the region. Therefore, it is worth noting here for the concerned authorities to look into the matter and meet the necessity

Table 4.22

Variable No. 22	1 Y	2 N	$\overline{X}$	St. Dev	Skew	Kurt	X^2	P. Value
Do you get newspaper regularly?	56	144	1.72	.453	-1.011	-1.021	9.68	<0.05

Source : Field Survey, data collected through interview schedules circulated among respondents.

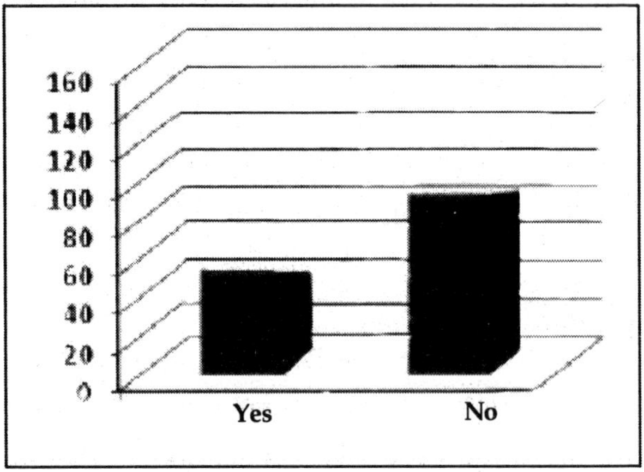

The life of modern man starts with the reading of newspapers and watching of national channels for news and entertainment. It is only through media, especially newspaper, that people come to know about the development activities and information about government policies and decisions. Through this means only they develop opinions about ruling agencies and express their views which work as feedback to the government. The absence of such provision is a big hiccup in the evolution of an area.

What if the said services are not available to the residents of a particular region? How long can we curse geography and nature for this? It is a sad tale for the region of Ladakh since only 28% of the respondents approved of having newspapers in their areas. A good majority within this group belongs to urban respondents. About 72% respondents had no newspapers in their areas and this speaks of the huge lag that the region is having vis-a-vis the other two regions. It is not that this is untrue of the other regions (especially tribal areas of other states) but in a state that has undergone political upheavals over the decades and a region so perceptive about its protection and development, the factor adds fuel to the discontent. The service can be improvised only when there is a good road network and transportation service. This is another area of consideration for the state government.

Table 4.23

Variable No. 22	1 Y	2 N	$\overline{X}$	St. Dev	Skew	Kurt	X^2	P. Value
Do you have banking facility?	136	64	1.32	4.71	.796	-1.425	6.48	<0.05

Source : Field Survey, data collected through interview schedules circulated among respondents.

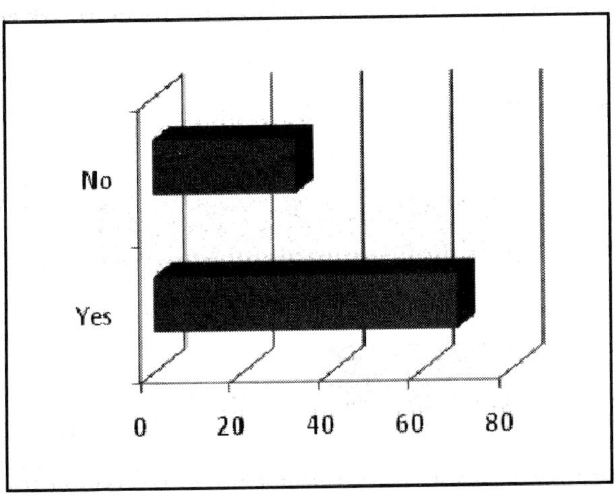

The economy of an area is evaluated with the help of indicators like per capita income, investments, commerce, trade, industries and savings of the people. Banks reflect the true economic picture of an area. About 68% respondents affirmed that they had banking facility in their village or area. 32% respondents, however, denied any such facility. Since the region is not well developed in roads and transportation and has very small number of industries the savings of the people are small and banks are consequently less in number. Taken into account the nature and geography and compared to other such regions of India the number of banks in the region are not too disappointing.

Table 4.24

Variable No. 24	1 Y	2 N	$\overline{X}$	St. Dev	Skew	Kurt	X^2	P. Value
Are there industries in your area?	60	140	1.70	.462	-.900	-1.241	8.00	<0.05

Source : Field Survey, data collected through interview schedules circulated among respondents.

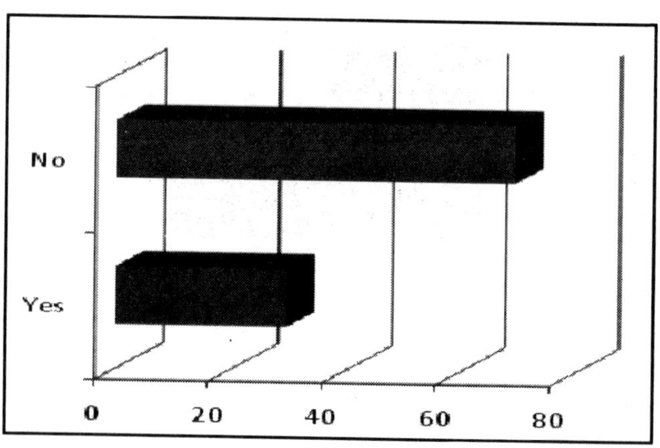

Industry is an important signifier and indicator of development of a region. It is an established fact that development of industry largely depends on the availability of good infrastructure like roads, electricity, railway, means of communication and natural resources. Raw material and access of market are other important prerequisites for industry. In an area where all these basic requirements are present the industrial sector has flourished and more we deviate from these basics lesser would be the presence of industry. Industry is significant primarily on account of production, marketing and source of employment. Industrially developed areas are centres of employment.

Asked about whether there are industries in your area, 70% respondents replied in negative while only 30% respondents approved with the presence of industry in their area. Besides this the small industries which are there in the region are primarily located in the towns of Leh and Kargil. Besides tourism and hotel industry the DICs of the region have mostly registered small industries in the fields of handicrafts, handloom, embroidery, fruit processing, weaving, carpet weaving, clay moulding, wood carving etc.

Therefore, the study reveals that the region of Ladakh has many grounds on which it has developed a sense of deprivation and feels estranged from the other two regions. They not only hold their separate cultural identity but feel that in the changed global scenario it is waning and feel challenged by the forces of the time. The youth seems to be indifferent towards the culture and traditions of Ladakh and the social structure is getting non-stringent. The process of globalization that fillips the consciousness level and living standards of the people has on the one hand caused identity loss while on the other helped widen the rift between the two sub-regions of Kargil and Leh in Ladakh. Even in educational and medical institutions, Ladakhis express annoyance over the non-availability of sufficient teachers, medicines and doctors. The same is true of banks and telecommunications. People also express worry over non-availability of drinkable water and electricity in many areas, a cause of concern for them. All the areas are not connected by roads and most of them are fair-weather non-metalled roads, which is again a source of discontent among people. Lack of capital investment and consequent evolution of industrial sector that is causative of employment generation is yet another area of concern. Thus Ladakhis have a long list of grievances on which they can count upon for expressing anguish with the current state of affairs.

Chapter 5

Inter-Regional Divergence and Ladakh-II

(Administrative, Legislative and Political)

If social and economic factors have a substantial role to play in the regional divergence the political factors such as nature of governance, share in political cake, discrimination in development related activities, power and institutional differentiation are equally significant. If increase of wealth and living standards of people signify prosperity and development and evolution of secularism minimise the societal disparities, the formation of democratic institutions and rise in political participation reflect development at political level.

The shaping of group aspirations, looking for betterment in life standards and prosperity might take place on numerous grounds. There can be economic opportunities that show an improved state of life, cultural disparities that lend inbuilt divergences, development lag that might provide a plank for public manoeuvres or political grievances which open up newer vistas of imagined destinies yet to be realised.

Theoretically too, it has been observed, that the presence of staunch dominant ethnic group in a state that tries to dictate the terms because of an advantageous position also consolidates the counter-currents among the disadvantageous groups. And if such advantageous groups are at the same time eloquent about secessionist moves or tend to profess inclination towards separatism stronger would be the feelings of segregation among the other groups.

In the current chapter we intend to investigate the political factors which might have played a significant role in the formation or evolution of regional feelings among the people of Ladakh vis-á-vis Jammu and Kashmir. The state has undergone political change over the decades so far as institutional and power devolution is concerned. The grant of tribal status and Ladakh Autonomous Hill Development Councils for the region of Ladakh has also influenced the regional opinion. Yet, much needs to be done as the Ladakhis show a sense of insecurity and deprivation which is revealed in the ensuing analysis.

When put to the question that Ladakhis are discriminated by state government administratively and economically a good majority of them approve with the statement. See Table No. 5.1.

Table 5.1

Variable 1	1 SD	2 D	3 PA	4 A	5 SA	$\overline{X}$	St. Dev	Skew	Kurt	X^2	P Value
There is discrimination with the region by the state governments at the administrative and economic level		44	16	12	128	4.12	1.27	-.915	-1.010	43.60	<0.05

Source : Field Survey, data collected through interview schedules circulated among respondents.

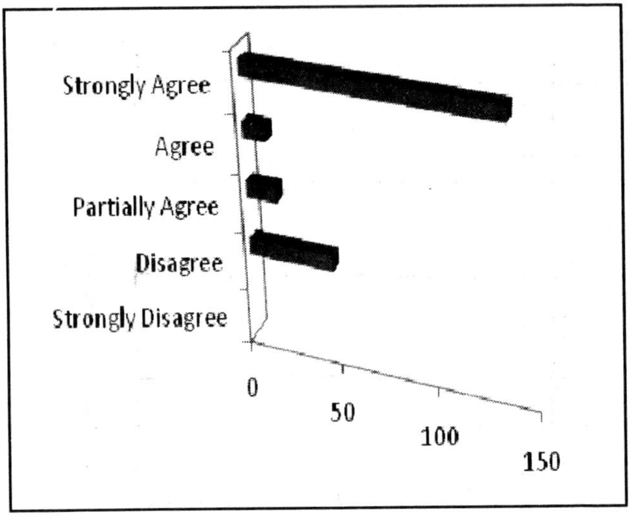

The opinion of the respondents regarding the variable 'there is discrimination with the region by the state governments at the administrative and economic level' reveals that the mean value of the opinion is more than the standard average. The variation in the opinion is 1.27 and skewness is recorded at -.915 that shows the scattering of the data towards higher side. While applying X^2 test of goodness at fit it rejects the null hypothesis at 5% level of significance. It shows that the distribution of opinion is unequal. Thus the above analysis leads us to conclude that the respondents strongly agree with the fact that there is discrimination with the region by the state governments at the administrative and economic level. It has been observed previously too that Ladakhis have expressed their anguish time and again over the issues of unemployment, less representation in government and poor devolution of funds.

Table 5.2

Variable 2	1 Y	2 N	$\overline{X}$	St. Dev	Skew	Kurt	X^2	P. Value
Are you happy with the grant of Scheduled Tribe status to the people of Ladakh	200	–	100	0.00	–	–	–	<0.05

Source : Field Survey, data collected through interview schedules circulated among respondents.

Partaining to the variable "Are you happy with the grant of Scheduled Tribe Status to the people of Ladakh" the respondents' opinion is quite unilinear since all the respondents believe that the grant of Tribal Status to Ladakh has pacified the people of Ladakh to a great extent since it helps them in many ways. In fact this was for quite a long time the demand of LBA. The grant of Scheduled Tribe status at least ensures more devolution of funds on account of development heads from both State and Union Governments. Therefore, Ladakhis would in no way resist the grant of the Status.

Table 5.3

Variable 3	1 SD	2 D	3 PA	4 A	5 SA	$\overline{X}$	St. Dev	Skew	Kurt	X^2	P·Value
You get sufficient grants from the state governments on account of develop-ment	16	112	24	32	16	2.60	1.10	.866	-.217	41.6	<0.05

Source : Field Survey, data collected through interview schedules circulated among respondents.

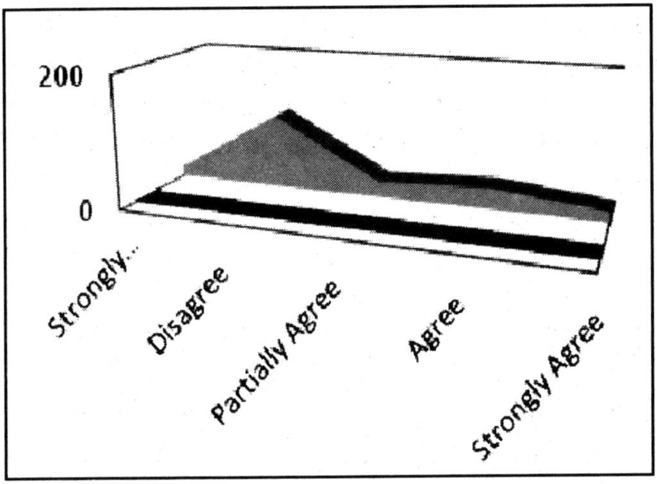

The prime source of finance of a region within a state system is normally the grants and development funds it receives from its government. More the flow of assistance, more the development activities take place in the area and the vice versa. The people here seem to be strongly disappointed over the flow of this assistance and feel discriminated by the state government especially when the state of Jammu and Kashmir happens to be the largest recipient of the Union assistance when compared to other states of its size and proportion like Himachal, Uttarakhand or Punjab.

While asked about the related variable "You get sufficient grants from the state governments on account of development" the answer of the respondents reveals that the mean value of the opinion is more than the standard average. The variation in the opinion is 1.10 and skewness is recorded at .866 that shows the scattering of the data towards lower side. Kurtosis recorded at -.217. The application of X^2 test of goodness at fit rejects the null hypothesis at 5% level of significance. It shows that the distribution of opinion is unequal. Thus the above analysis leads us to conclude that the respondents strongly agree with the fact that not only is there discrimination with the region at the administrative and economic levels but even at the level of devolution of finance. The state government is advised to take into consideration the development lag of the region and devolve more sources towards the development heads of the region.

Table 5.4

Variable 3	1 SD	2 D	3 PA	4 A	5 SA	$\overline{X}$	St. Dev	Skew	Kurt	X^2	P-Value
The relations between the people of Kargil and Leh are smooth	8	20	44	76	52	3.72	1.088	-.694	-.053	18.00	<0.05

Source : Field Survey, data collected through interview schedules circulated among respondents.

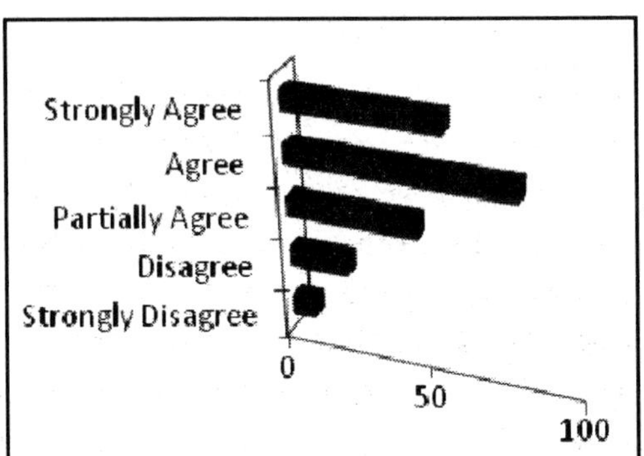

Since the region of Ladakh is again divisible into two different sub-regions of Leh and Kargil and the two regions have significant variation over communal composition, it has been observed that this factor has influenced the regional perceptions of the people there. It is largely believed that since Kargil is a Muslim majority area it sides with Valley on the alternative options of the region outside the state. In fact this has been observed that the respondents who tend to stay with Jammu & Kashmir and oppose separate UT status belong to Kargil. This sometimes brings more acrimony into the mutuality of relations between the people of the two sub-regions. The respondents although negate the said fear over the concerned variable yet a significant part of them strongly believes that the relations are not as smooth as they are believed to be by many.

Regarding the variable "The relations between the people of Kargil and Leh are smooth" the respondents' reply demonstrates that the mean value of the opinion is more than the standard average. The variation in the opinion is 1.088 and skewness is recorded at -.694 that shows the scattering of the data towards upper side. Kurtosis recorded at -.053 shows that the opinion is of mesokurtic nature. The application of X^2 test of goodness at fit rejects the null hypothesis at 5% level of significance. It shows that the distribution of opinion is unequal. The above analysis reveals that the respondents agree with the fact that the relations between the people of Leh and Kargil are quite smooth. However, 14% respondents denies the fact and 22% respondents partially believe that the relations are not so smooth. Therefore, there seems to be something more than mere cordiality in the relations among the people of Leh and Kargil.

Table 5.5

Variable 5	1 SD	2 D	3 PA	4 A	5 SA	$\overline{X}$	St. Dev	Skew	Kurt	X^2	P Value
The People of Leh and Kargil districts have separate social and cultural traditions and they deserve separate treatment	4	76	20	28	72	3.44	1.37	-.017	-1.733	18.00	<0.05

Source : Field Survey, data collected through interview schedules circulated among respondents.

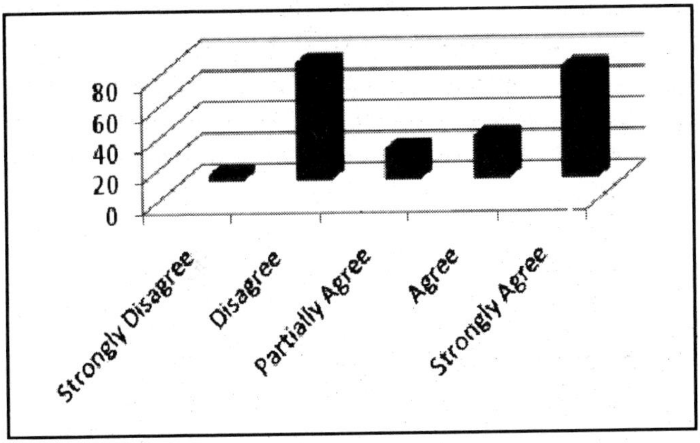

There are lots of common points between the people of two sub-regions. However, a lot more is there that distinguish them from each other. About the variable "The people of Leh and Kargil districts have separate social and cultural traditions and they deserve separate treatment" the opinion of the respondents is widely divided. It shows that the mean value of the opinion is more than the standard average. The variation in the opinion is 1.37 and skewness is recorded at -.017 that shows the scattering of the data towards upper side. Kurtosis recorded at -1.733 shows that the opinion is of platikurtik nature. The application of X^2 test of goodness at fit rejects the null hypothesis at 5% level of significance. It shows that the distribution of opinion is unequal. The above analysis reveals that majority of the respondents agree with the fact that the people of Leh and Kargil districts have separate social and cultural traditions. However, 40% respondents deny the fact and 10% respondents partially deny the distinctivity of traditions and culture thus leaving enough space for consideration over the factor.

This shows that a big portion of people still believe that the people of Kargil and Leh are socially and culturally a cohesive unit and efforts at their segregation are unwelcome. However, since Kargilites are predominantly Muslims and people of Leh Buddhists and they have lingual variations too, the two sub-regions have their own distinct identities too.

Table 5.6

Variable 6	1 SD	2 D	3 PA	4 A	5 SA	$\overline{X}$	St. Dev	Skew	Kurt	X^2	P.Value
The phenomenon of insurgency in the valley has tensed the relations of people of Ladakh vis-a vis the people of Valley	8	32	56	56	48	3.52	1.147	-.304	-.759	10.04	<0.05

Source : Field Survey, data collected through interview schedules circulated among respondents.

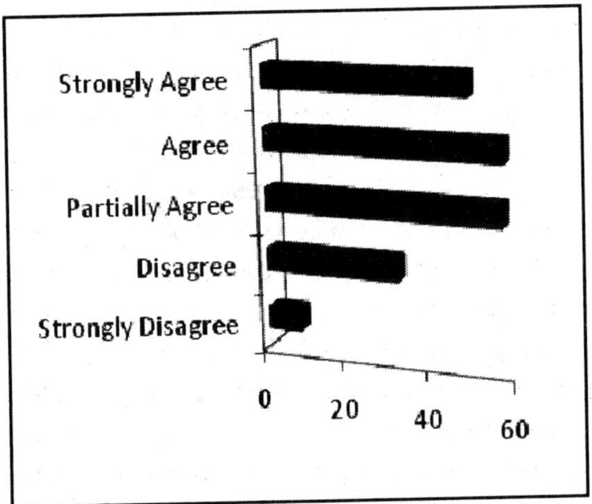

It is also believed that the phenomenon of insurgency has also played upon the sentiments of the people of Kargil and Leh adversely. Since the valley based terrorism has its communal overtones and is targeted against a specific community its repercussions on the bilateral relations between the people of two sub-regions are imminent. Although, Ladakh is a Buddhist majority region yet the over-harping of the communal forces about the status of the state make the people here sceptical.

In response to the variable "The phenomenon of insurgency in the valley has tensed the relations of people of Ladakh vis-a-vis the people of Valley" the majority of the respondents are of the view that 'yes' it has tensed the relations. The reply demonstrates that the mean value of the opinion is more than the standard average. The variation in the opinion is 1.147 and skewness is recorded at -.304 that shows the scattering of the data towards upper side. Kurtosis recorded at -.759 shows that the opinion is of platikurtic nature. The application of X^2 test of goodness at fit rejects the null hypothesis at 5% level of significance.

It shows that the distribution of opinion is unequal. Thus the analysis reveals that again there is a huge difference in the perception of the respondents regarding the impact of insurgency over the people of the region. Where 52% respondents agree with the statement about 20% repudiate it However, a big chunk of 28% respondents partially agrees with the development. There is a close nexus between the current and the previous variable where 22% respondents partially believe that the relations between the people of the two regions are unwell. Therefore, it is safe to argue that one of the prime reasons behind the regional divergence of the people of Ladakh vis-a-vis the other two regions and intra-regional pulls is the job of insurgency that lends a sense of insecurity and identity crisis in the region.

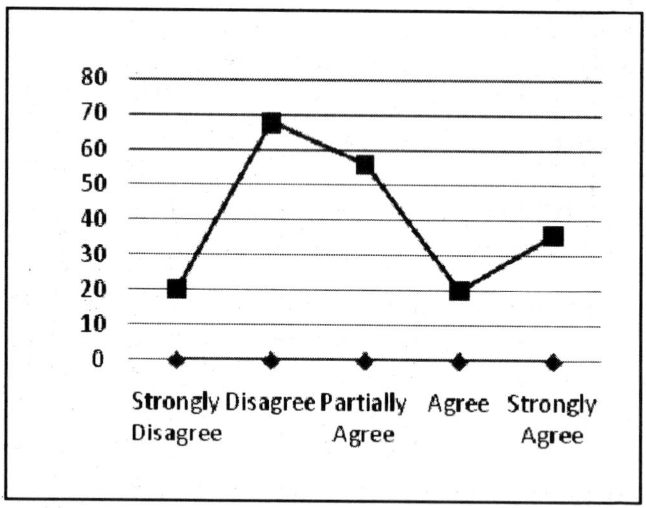

Table 5.7

Variable 7	1 SD	2 D	3 PA	4 A	5 SA	$\overline{X}$	St. Dev	Skew	Kurt	X^2	P.Value
Insurgency in the valley has influenced the opinion of the people of Ladakh vis-a-vis India	20	68	56	20	36	2.92	1.25	.412	-.849	11.60	<0.05

Source : Field Survey, data collected through interview schedules circulated among respondents.

Insurgency seems to have a role in the development of the sense of alienation among Ladakhis with the Union government on the one hand and the state government on the other. It not only physically harms people but creates psychological clefts among them. Such distances are irreparable as has been observed over militancy affected regions of the world. The hypothesis has been partially verified here.

About the variable "Insurgency in the valley has influenced the opinion of the people of Ladakh vis-a-vis India" the respondents' opinion is again widely spread over the multi-scales. The answer by respondents expresses that the mean value of the opinion is more than the standard average. The variation in the opinion is 1.25 and skewness is recorded at .412 that shows the slight scattering of the data towards lower side. Kurtosis recorded at -.849 shows that the opinion is of mesokurtic nature. The application of X^2 test of goodness at fit rejects the null hypothesis at 5% level of significance. It shows that the distribution of opinion is unequal. The above analysis reveals that 44% of the respondents disagree with the statement that the insurgency has influenced the opinion of the people of Ladakh. However, 28% respondents approve with the statement while another 28% partially agree. Here if we take the majority opinion then insurgency has nothing to do with the regional stance of the people of Ladakh. However, a big section believes that yes it has influenced the opinion. Therefore, we have to partially admit that insurgency has its inroads into the hearts of the people of Ladakh now and more peaceful the valley more stable the regions of the state. Theoretically too, it is believed that if a group which is in advantageous position goes violent in a state it tacitly reinforces the counter feelings in other people of the state and divergence takes more acrid shapes if such groups carry separate distinct identities.

Table 5.8

Variable 8	1 SD	2 D	3 PA	4 A	5 SA	$\overline{X}$	St. Dev	Skew	Kurt	X^2	P.Value
The separate cultural identity of Ladakh could be protected only in an independent political identity (Separate State or Union Territory)	–	48	8	28	116	4.06	1.26	-.867	-1.1042	33.04	<0.05

Source : Field Survey, data collected through interview schedules circulated among respondents.

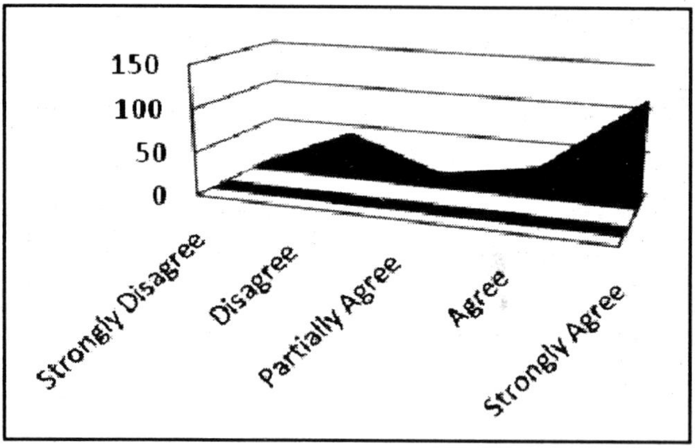

Ladakh has a long history of struggle for an independent political status be it Union Territory or separate state. The initial struggle led by Kushak Bakula is still alive and efforts at pacifying the demand for separate state or UT have not worked well. It seems to be an unfinished agenda on part of Ladakh Buddhist Association and Congress. The grant of Scheduled Tribe status to the people of Ladakh and Ladakh and Kargil Autonomous Hill Councils has, though, to some extent pacified the discontent but the people are still in favour of segregation of the region from the rest of state. Peace, development and projection of separate identity can be the chief force behind this.

Regarding the view that the separate cultural identity of Ladakh could be protected only in an independent political identity (Separate State or Union Territory) the respondents' opinion is preponderantly in favour of grant of separate statehood or Union Territory for the region. The answer by respondents reveals that the mean value of the opinion is more than the standard average. The variation in the opinion is 1.26 and skewness is recorded at -.867 that shows the scattering of the data towards upper side. Kurtosis recorded at -1.042 shows that the opinion is of platikurtic nature. The application of X^2 test of goodness at fit rejects the null hypothesis at 5% level of significance. It shows that the distribution of opinion is unequal. The above analysis reveals that a good majority of the respondents (72%) agree with the opinion that if the culture and traditions of the region are to be safeguarded the best alternate way is to make them self dependent and decisive with the grant of separate statehood or UT status.

However, 24% respondents are not in favour of this kind of relaxation and it is interesting to note here that about 8% of respondents who don't want separate statehood belong to Kargil region. It is interesting to note here that while the Muslims of Leh would prefer to stay with Buddhists and plead for separate UT status the Muslims of Kargil would prefer to align with Valley. This further makes clear that there is difference of perception about the future of region even within the people of Ladakh. While the sub-region of Leh is preponderantly in favour of separate UT status, the people of Kargil are more in favour of staying with the valley.

Table 5.9

Variable No. 9	1 Y	2 N	$\overline{X}$	St. Dev	Skew	Kurt	X^2	P. Value
Are you aware of article 370 of the constitution of India?	176	24	1.12	.328	2.412	3.974	–	<0.05

Source : Field Survey, data collected through interview schedules circulated among respondents.

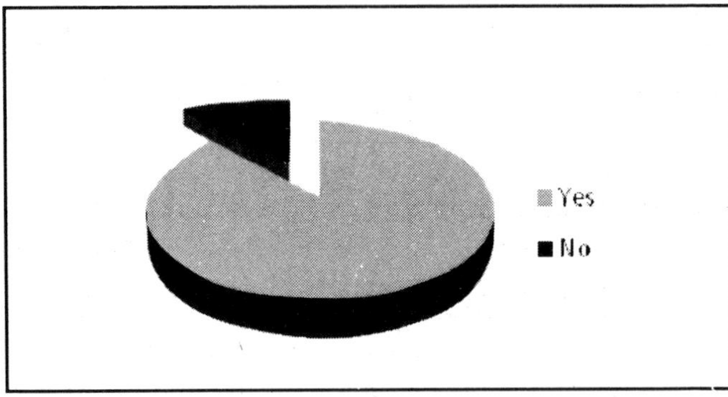

The Constitution of India provides a special status to the state of Jammu and Kashmir under Article 370. Under this article the state enjoys several privileges which the other Indian states don't enjoy e.g separate constitution, separate flag, separate citizenship and many more. However, the constitution of Jammu and Kashmir fails to meet the regional aspirations because of its unitary character. The less devolution of powers to the other two regions has time and again led to protests and regional tensions.

To observe the general awareness of the people regarding the article, the variable "Are you aware of Article 370 of the constitution of India" was framed. Since the rate of literacy is not high many of the respondents (about 12%) were found unaware of the provision. The respondent's opinion reveals that the mean value of the opinion is more than the standard average. The variation in the opinion is .328 and skewness is recorded at 2.412 that shows the scattering of the data towards upper side. Kurtosis has been recorded at 3.974. The application of X^2 test of goodness at fit rejects the null hypothesis at 5% level of significance. It shows that the distribution of opinion is unequal. The above analysis reveals that a good majority of the respondents (88%) are well aware of the constitutional provision of Article 370.

Table 5.10

Variable 10	1 SD	2 D	3 PA	4 A	5 SA	$\overline{X}$	St. Dev	Skew	Kurt	X^2	P·Value
Airticle 370 of the Constitution of India should be retained	36	16	16	56	76	3.60	1.51	-.753	-.935	17.00	<0.05

Source : Field Survey, data collected through interview schedules circulated among respondents.

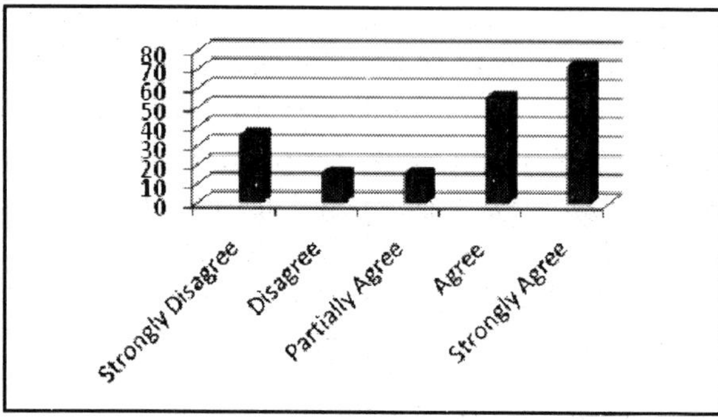

There has been a huge debate since beginning throughout India regarding the retention or suspension of Article 370 of the constitution. Since rest of the states don't have that privileged position they regard it as discriminatory to them. Contrary to its abolition many of the states have even advocated devolution of more financial powers to them. However, keeping the debate aside the people of the region of Ladakh seem to be quite conscious over the special status under article 370 and would not allow any proposition that weakens it.

When asked whether "Article 370 of the Constitution of India should be retained" a good majority of them opted for its retention. The respondent's opinion here shows that the mean value of the opinion is more than the standard average. The variation in the opinion is 1.51 and skewness is recorded at -.753 that shows the scattering of the data towards upper side. Kurtosis recorded at -.935 shows that the opinion is of platikurtic nature. The application of X^2 test of goodness at fit rejects the null hypothesis at 5% level of significance. It shows that the distribution of opinion is unequal. The above analysis reveals that a majority of the respondents (66%) are in favour of the retention of Article 370. Although 26% respondents are in favour of its abolition which refers to a significant discontent against the provision yet the voice for its retention is louder. Partially this seems to be there because the region longs for a separate statehood or UT status and they won't compromise what they have achieved right now. Although the opinion here is contrary to the one of separate state or UT status yet it strengthens the view that Ladakhis won't let frisk away the autonomy and special status that they enjoy under Article 370.

Table 5.11

Variable No. 11	1 Y	2 N	$\overline{X}$	St. Dev	Skew	Kurt	X^2	P. Value
Are you happy with the nature and the structure of the constitution of Jammu and Kashmir	156	44	1.22	.418	1.394	-.061	15.68	<0.05

Source : Field Survey, data collected through interview schedules circulated among respondents.

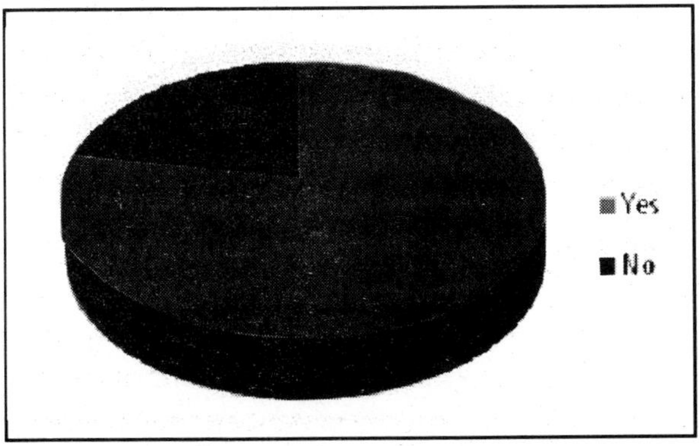

The Constitution of Jammu and Kashmir gives the people a sense of special attention and pride. They may differ over its nature and unitary character yet they won't go against it at any cost. Though, the people of the region have grievances against the undue retention of leverage with the Valley yet they have come out whole heartedly in favour of the nature of their constitution. Partially this can be because of less awareness about the nature of government and its organization and the Constitution of Jammu and Kashmir but there seems to be a broader understanding about the Constitution.

In reply to the question "Are you happy with the nature and the structure of the Constitution of Jammu and Kashmir?" the opinion of the respondents shows that the mean value of the opinion is more than the standard average. The variation in the opinion is .418 and skewness is recorded at -1.394 that shows the scattering of the data towards upper side. Kurtosis is recorded at -.061. The application of X^2 test of goodness at fit rejects the null hypothesis at 5% level of significance. It shows that the distribution of opinion is unequal. The above analysis reveals that a majority of the respondents (78%) have no problem with the nature of the Constitution of Jammu and Kashmir. Although 28% respondents are unhappy with the character of the constitution yet it has to be observed that when people of the region are looking for separate statehood why they conform to the unitary character of the constitution. The only probability seems to be ignorance about the nature and organization of the Constitution of State.

Table 5.12

Variable 12	1 SD	2 D	3 PA	4 A	5 SA	$\overline{X}$	St. Dev	Skew	Kurt	X^2	P.Value
The process of globalization has increased the political conscious-ness level of the people	–	–	32	116	52	4.10	.646	-.094	-.525	14.44	<0.05

Source : Field Survey, data collected through interview schedules circulated among respondents.

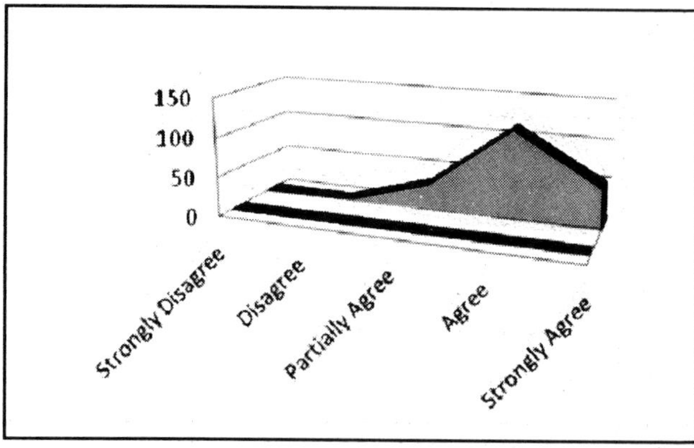

In this global era the spate of information and the flow of goods have brought a significant transformation in the societies. We are witness to tremendous changes in social structures and consumer habits which of course go on to influence the fundamentals of a culture too. It is an established fact that the people world over are now concerned about the severing of cultural texture because of the erosion of the cultural values due to the advent of material culture of consumerism. The impact of the globalisation process has been noticed in the far flung areas of the country and this seems to be true of the region of Ladakh also.

In response to the statement "The process of globalization has increased the political consciousness level of the people" the respondents have preponderantly accepted the phenomenon. The respondent's opinion shows that the mean value is more than the standard average. The variation in the opinion is .646 and skewness is recorded at -.094 that shows the scattering of the data towards upper side. Kurtosis recorded at -.525 shows that the opinion is of mesokurtic nature.

The application of X^2 test of goodness at fit rejects the null hypothesis at 5% level of significance. It shows that the distribution of opinion is unequal. This is evident from the analysis that the people of Ladakh are unanimous about the advent of consumer culture and the vices of globalization acting upon the local values and culture.

Table 5.13

Variable No. 13	1 Y	2 N	$\bar{X}$	St. Dev	Skew	Kurt	X^2	P. Value
Are you happy with the founding of Ladakh Autonomous Hill Council?	192	8	1.04	.197	4.841	22.33	43.32	<0.05

Source : Field Survey, data collected through interview schedules circulated among respondents.

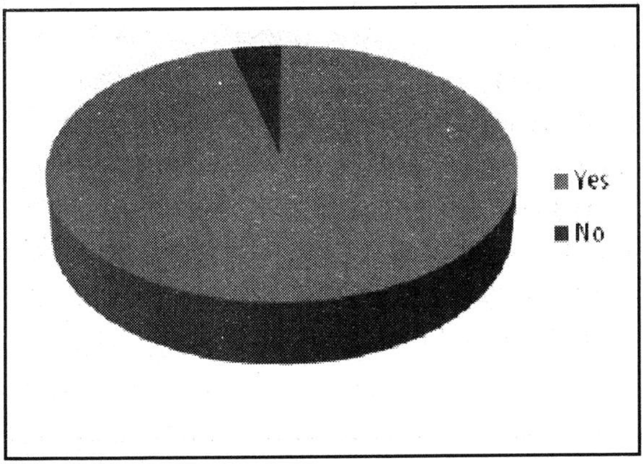

Demands for more regional autonomy and its continuous quest have remained central to all the federal systems of the world. In India also we have witnessed such demands and agitations time and again. In the state of Jammu and Kashmir the regions of Jammu and Ladakh have been engaged in such agitations since the promulgation of state constitution in 1951. In order to pacify such demands of the region of Ladakh, a Ladakh Autonomus Hill Development Council was announced for Leh area in 1995. This was followed by a similar grant to the region of Kargil. It is believed that the formation of such autonomous bodies would meet the regional aspirations of the people and devolve a sense of autonomy and power decentralisation. The current variable seeks to garner the opinion of the respondents about the grant of these councils.

Asked about whether the people are happy with the founding of the Ladakh Autonomous Hill Council almost all the respondents have preponderantly shown happiness over the grant. The respondent's opinion shows that the mean value is more than the standard average. The variation in the opinion is. 197 and skewness is recorded at 4.841that shows the scattering of the data towards higher side. Kurtosis is recorded at 22.31. The application of X^2 test of goodness at fit rejects the null hypothesis at 5% level of significance. It shows that the distribution of opinion is unequal. This is evident from the analysis that the people of Ladakh are happy with the grant of Hill Development Council and consider this development as a milestone towards achieving a better political status.

Table 5.14

Variable 14	1 SD	2 D	3 PA	4 A	5 SA	$\overline{X}$	St. Dev	Skew	Kurt	X^2	P.Value
Ladakh Autonomous Hill Council meets the requirements of the People		24	80	80	16	3.44	.812	.037	-.425	18.16	<0.05

Source : Field Survey, data collected through interview schedules circulated among respondents.

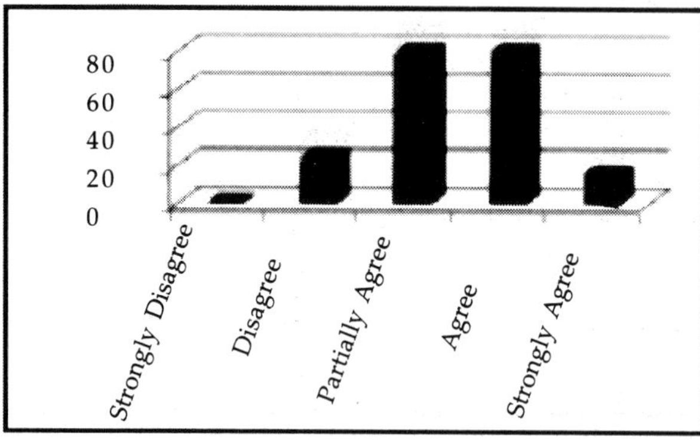

Although, the people of the region are happy regarding the grant of Hill development Councils yet they seem to differ over the functioning and performance of the councils. With the grant of councils it was believed that the people of the two sub-regions of Ladakh would have more say in governance and they would register more economic development. However, it seems from the current analysis that the councils have failed to perform the job they were expected.

In reference to the variable "whether the Ladakh Autonomous Hill Council meet the requirements of the people" the response appears to be widely scattered on five scale options. A slight majority of the respondents (48%) have shown satisfaction over the performance of the council. The respondent's opinion shows that the mean value is more than the standard average. The variation in the opinion is .812 and skewness is recorded at .037 that shows the scattering of the data towards higher side. Kurtosis recorded at -.425 shows that the opinion is of mesokurtic nature. The application of X^2 test of goodness at fit rejects the null hypothesis at 5% level of significance. It shows that the distribution of opinion is unequal. This is evident from the analysis that majority of the people of

Ladakh are happy with the performance of the Council. However, a big section of the respondents (40%) are in 'cant say' position which shows the suspense of the people over the functioning of the council. 12 % respondents are not happy with the achievements of the Council. This is associated with the devolution of powers to councils which most of the Ladakhis look for.

Table 5.15

Variable 15	1 SD	2 D	3 PA	4 A	5 SA	$\overline{X}$	St. Dev	Skew	Kurt	X^2	P.Value
Sufficient powers have been devolved to Ladakh Autonomous Hill Development Council and the people of Ladakh enjoy a great deal of autonomy now	8	52	80	44	16	3.4	.988	.181	-.341	21.00	<0.05

Source : Field Survey, data collected through interview schedules circulated among respondents.

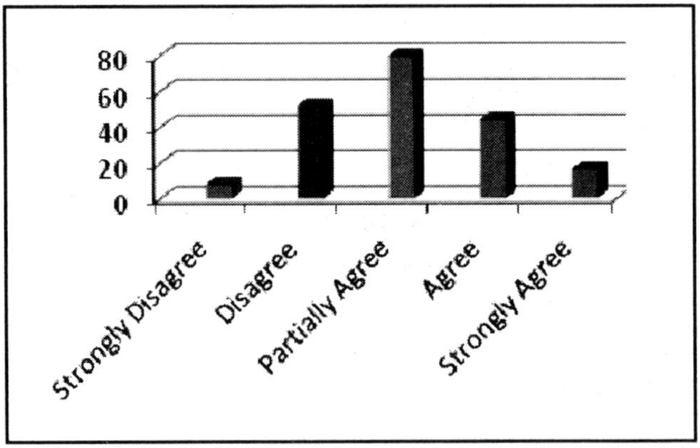

The autonomous councils carry meaning so far they are granted sufficient economic and political powers. Regarding the devolution of powers to councils again the opinion seems to be splintered. Asked whether "Sufficient powers have been devolved to Ladakh Autonomous Hill Development Council and the people of Ladakh enjoy a great deal of autonomy now" the opinion of the respondents is equipoised so far as 30% respondents register their opinion in agreement and disagreement. It is interesting to note that 40% respondents are in 'can't say' (ambivalent) position.

The respondent's opinion shows that the mean value is more than the standard average. The variation in the opinion is .988 and skewness is recorded at .181 that shows the scattering of the data towards higher side. Kurtosis recorded at -.341shows that the opinion is of makes sharp top mesokurtic nature. The application of X^2 test of goodness at fit rejects the null hypothesis at 5% level of significance. It shows that the distribution of opinion is unequal. This is evident from the analysis that there is no unanimity of opinion regarding the variable since equal number of respondents are in agreement or disagreement about the devolution of sufficient powers to the council. It shows that the people are still looking for more devolving of powers to the councils and the state government is advised to look into the issue and see which other important heads could be transferred in councils' way.

Table 5.16

Variable 16	1 Y	2 N		St. Dev	Skew	Kurt	X^2	P. Value
Do you vote	200	Nil	1.00	.0000	–	–	–	–

Source : Field Survey, data collected through interview schedules circulated among respondents.

In a democracy it is the vote that counts. More the participation in the political process by people more successful the democracy is. The exercise of the right to vote by the voters is the prime criterion that tells about the state of participation and political consciousness level of the people. Regarding the people of the region of Ladakh it is nice to find that all the respondents have shown keen interest about the use of voting right. Though in most of the elections the participation rate has not been so high yet all the respondents have agreed that they cast vote. When asked whether they vote all the respondents (100%) have affirmatively held that yes, they vote. Thus it is evident from the analysis that all the respondents take it as a matter of pride to exercise the right to vote since not a single respondent replied in negative.

Table 5.17

Variable 17	1 SD	2 D	3 PA	4 A	5 SA	$\overline{X}$	St. Dev	Skew	Kurt	X^2	P·Value
The people participate in large numbers in the elections of Halqa Panchayats, State Legistative Assembly, Ladakh Autonomous Hill Development Council and Parliament	–	–	40	68	92	4.26	.777	-.497	-1.161	5.080	<0.05

Source : Field Survey, data collected through interview schedules circulated among respondents.

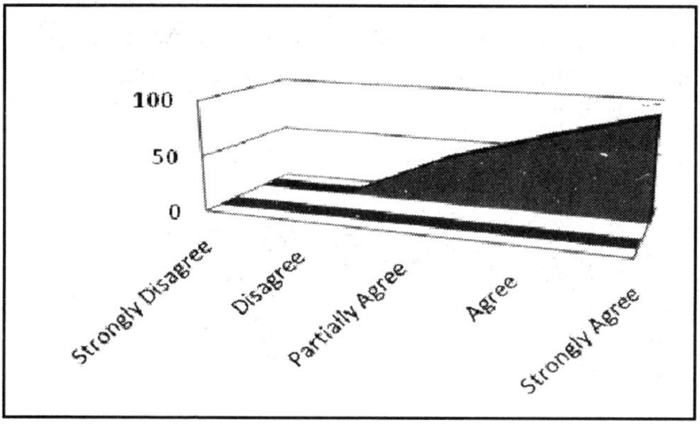

Related with the previous question, another question was posed regarding the participation of the people in elections at different levels. The respondents seem to be enthusiastic about their electoral participation as a good majority of them again replied in affirmative 'yes'. Asked about whether people participate in large numbers in the elections of Halqa Panchayats, State Legislative Assembly, Ladakh Autonomous Hill Development Council and Parliament, the opinion of the respondents shows that the mean value is more than the standard average. The variation in the opinion is .777 and skewness is recorded at -.497 that shows the scattering of the data towards higher side. Kurtosis recorded at -1.161 shows that the opinion is of makes sharp top mesokurtic nature. The application of X^2 test of goodness at fit rejects the null hypothesis at 5% level of significance. It shows that the distribution of opinion is unequal. This is evident from the analysis that a vast majority of the respondents are of the view that yes they participate in electoral process at different levels of democratic institutions. Only 20% respondents are in partial agreement with none in disagreement about such participation. The registration of such a vast majority over electoral participation establishes that the level of political consciousness among Ladakhis is quite high and democracy percolates to the remotest of the areas of region.

Table 5.18

Variable 18	1 SD	2 D	3 PA	4 A	5 SA	$\overline{X}$	St. Dev	Skew	Kurt	X^2	P.Value
Ladakh has got sufficient repesentation in the State Legislative Assembly and Ministry.	52	104	12	16	16	2.20	1.16	1.224	.826	38.60	<0.05

Source : Field Survey, data collected through interview schedules circulated among respondents.

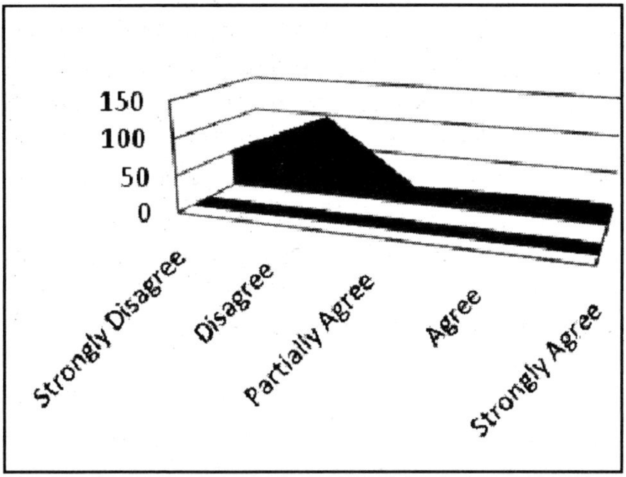

Regional representation in the Council of Ministers and State Legislative Assembly has been one of the significant issues in state-region pull over the years. The people of Ladakh have been demanding more shares in state ministries and more seats in the state legislative Assembly and this issue has caused a lot of embarrassment to the state government.

It is apparent from the opinion of the respondents regarding the variable "Ladakh has got sufficient representation in the State Legislative Assembly and ministry" that the mean value (2.20) of the opinion is more than the standard average i.e. three at the five point scale. The variation in the opinion is 1.16 and skewness is recorded at -1.224 that shows the scattering of the data towards higher side. Kurtosis is recorded at .826. While applying X^2 test of goodness at fit it rejects the null hypothesis at 5% level of significance. It shows that the distribution of opinion is unequal.

Thus the above analysis leads us to conclude that the

respondents are broadly in disagreement with the statement that the region has been duly represented in the state assembly as well as in the council of ministers. Therefore, the state government is advised to have a look at the representation figures of the region. Here it is not necessary that the population data is taken as the sole criterion for the determination of assembly seats. Sometimes geography has its own assertions and it should be duly admitted. The problems of a 50,000 people scattered over 15000 sq. kms. of an area are normally more acute than 5 lakh people residing in a territory of 1000 sq. kms. It is worth to mention here that no other region of India remains cut off from rest of the country for about 6 months except Ladakh since roads are crippled because of heavy snowfall after October every year and the reopening takes place around May next year. What if the region gets no development in this direction after 6 decades of independence of India? The State Government as well as the Union Government is required to pay necessary attention about these genuine regrets of the people of the region to pacify their feelings of negligence.

The idea of an independent unit within a federal set up may appeal to every person and it is no surprise if the people of a region like Ladakh look for the same. Autonomy itself is a substitute for development since it is believed that in a self governed region people have systems of checks and balances and they go for faster development than centrally governed units. The idea of Union Territory may fall short of these aspirations but this seems to be a step towards real autonomous status within the constitutional set up of India very much in line with the rest of the Indian states. The people of the region are curious about this and they want to continue with the long standing demand of LBA for the segregation of the region from Jammu and Kashmir and creation of a new State or Union Territory.

Table 5.19

Variable 19	1 SD	2 D	3 PA	4 A	5 SA	$\overline{X}$	St. Dev	Skew	Kurt	X^2	P·Value
Ladakhis still look (as part of their erstwhile struggle) for Union Territory status as the best alternative for better prospects of Ladakh	—	16	12	56	116	4.36	.920	-1.449	1.287	34%	<0.05

Source : Field Survey, data collected through interview schedules circulated among respondents.

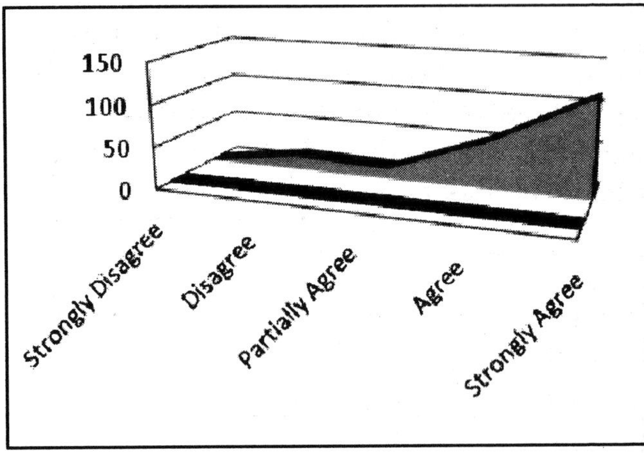

While probing over the regional view about the future status of the region it becomes evident that a vast majority of them want segregation of the region from the state of Jammu and Kashmir. Placed against the variable "Ladakhis still look (as part of their erstwhile struggle) for Union Territory status as the best alternative for better prospects of Ladakh" it becomes clear from the Table No. 5.19 that the mean value (4.36) of the opinion is more than the standard average i.e. three at the five point scale. The variation in the opinion is 1.920 and skewness is recorded at -1.449 that shows the scattering of the data towards higher side. Kurtosis is recorded at 1.287. While applying X^2 test of goodness at fit it rejects the null hypothesis at 5% level of significance. It shows that the distribution of opinion is unequal.

Thus we can safely conclude from the above analysis that a vast majority of the respondents (86%) are broadly in agreement with the statement that the Ladakhis still look for Union Territory status as the best alternative for the betterment of Ladakh. About 8 % respondents are against the option (Kargilites). This shows that though Kargilite

Muslims don't see protection of separate cultural identity possible under UT only yet they believe that the demand for UT is the best solution for the region. Therefore, this seems to be the unfinished agenda of the most of the Ladakhis to have an independent status outside the ambit of Jammu and Kashmir.

Table 5.20

Variable 20	1 SD	2 D	3 PA	4 A	5 SA	$\overline{X}$	St. Dev	Skew	Kurt	X^2	P.Value
Are the people of Ladakh sceptical about the Chinese intentions over the region		64	28	32	76	3.60	1.29	-.141	-1.719	8.40	<0.05

Source : Field Survey, data collected through interview schedules circulated among respondents.

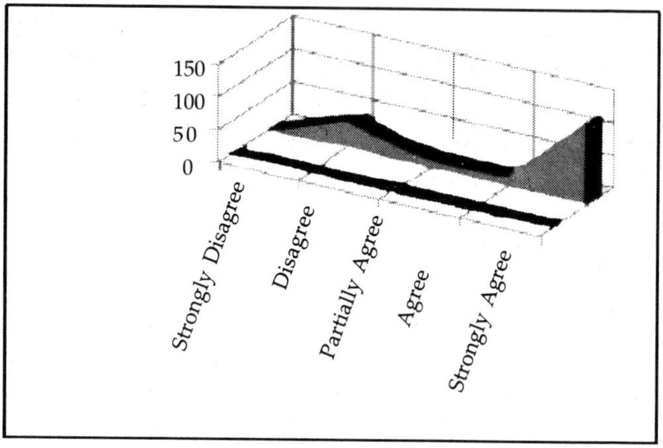

Ladakh is a region the part of which (Aksaichin) was annexed by the Peoples Republic of China in 1962. There are certain villages that the Ladakhis claim to be culturally their part and show strong angst against China over swallowing up of the same. It is a matter of great concern not only for India but to Ladakhis even that China still lays claim to the territories of Ladakh well to the south of Leh. Therefore, in the light of the consistent Chinese intrusions and border movements it is but natural to the people of the region to be suspicious over the Chinese intentions.

The statement "whether the people of Ladakh are sceptical about the Chinese intentions over the region" is ratisfied by a good majority of the respondents. The opinion of the respondents shows that the mean value 3.60 is more than the standard average i.e. three at the five point scale. The variation in the opinion is 1.29 and skewness is recorded at -.141 that shows the scattering of the data towards higher side. Kurtosis is recorded at -1.719. While applying X^2 test of goodness at fit it rejects the null hypothesis at 5% level of significance. It shows that the distribution of opinion is unequal. The above analysis reveals that the majority of the respondents are suspicious about the Chinese intentions in the region though 28% respondents are least concerned about Chinese moves over the border. Even most of the respondents would suggest the strengthening of the infrastructure built up in the region and deployment of more forces to plug any inflictions from Chinese side.

Therefore, it could well be ascertained that the political indicators behind the surge of Ladakhi discontent too have significant a role to play. Besides the social and cultural roles suppressed at the community level, a structure so strong in Ladakh, the state permeation and overtaking is bound to produce negatives from the governed side. It has been observed that hiccups in political participation, less representation in state executive, legislature and administration, protection of cultural identity, impact of globalizing forces, less devolution of powers to regional hill councils, unitary state constitution, discrimination at administrative and political level, and poor management of the region defence wise with the Chinese sword hanging like that of Damocles are the prime political factors that induce Ladakhis to look for better alternates which would end nothing short of a Union Territory status. They look for the better understanding of the problems of Ladakhis, of course as a community and not just as a political constituency, by the extension of services, power and finance so that the region can witness an era of tremendous change and development towards better life. Insurgency in the valley has also counter-strengthened the regional feelings in Ladakh and Jammu. Theoretically too, it has been observed globally that when an advantageous group in a state turns dominant and the other groups feel dictated they try to align against such dominant group, a phenomenon true of Jammu and Kashmir.

Concluding Remarks

One of the most important developments of the twentieth century has been the liquidation of colonialism and the emergence of a large number of states in Asia, Africa and Latin America. This development led to a great deal of optimism about the future of these countries in terms of national consolidation, modernization, state formation and industrialization. But there have been more failures than successes because nationalism in these countries came as a negative phenomenon. Unlike the Western states, where nationalism accompanied along industrial and democratic revolutions and where common culture and language were the key elements in the growth of nation-states, the new states of Asia, Africa and Latin America found the mixed seeds of their nationalism planted in essentially diverse social soils. Self-determination has become a major plank of the diverse communities in these states and India was no exception to it.

Unlike the West, the growth of state system in India took place very much like the developing states. Nationalism arose here mainly, as a reaction to the foreign rule and not as a positive phenomenon i.e. a process of internal assimilation and integration. It therefore failed to infuse a sense of unity in the Indian society, which is pluralistic in character. Pluralism lies principally in the diversities of our castes, creeds, religions, languages and ethnic origins and thus offers a tough resistance to the process of integration and synthesis. If the political arrangements are not sufficient to meet the aspirations of the people it is likely that people would look for more autonomy or separate political status within the state and even outside it. The process is further facilitated if the ethnically distinct community is concentrated at the border areas such as Punjab, Kashmir and North-Eastern States of India.

Federalism is considered to be a panacea for societies marred by diversities that beleaguer national unity. Theoretically, it is argued that a diverse group as a federating unit may bargain for more autonomy to maintain its distinct identity. The Indian federal system provides various provisions to solve its longstanding and intricate problems pertaining to the minorities, the backward classes, scheduled castes and tribes in a democratic manner. The maximum flexibility of the Indian federal system can be seen in the case of Jammu & Kashmir that enjoys special status. Thus the state alone involves a variation of the federal principles of the Indian Constitution.

The State of J & K is a miniature in India. It presents, at a relatively micro-level, the diversity of socio-economic, regional and religious and a pluralistic nature of the society that bears an important impact on the development within the state as also on its special relationships with the Government of India.

The processes of nation-building and national integration have been accompanied by the processes of modernization, development and globalization. These processes have helped eradicating the narrow parochial feelings of the people of India on the one hand but at the same we have witnessed the disintegrating effects of these processes too. The articulation of interests instead of being on expected class lines have also been noticed on narrow parochial lines, a phenomenon that can incapacitate a system to meet the challenges of different nature. The growth of ethnic nationalism prompted by such forces has marked the versatile developments in the relatively new societies with the integral fibre endangered. The case of Jammu and Kashmir is one of the kinds and the process further devolves to its regions of Jammu, Ladakh and Kashmir; thus accentuating the regional diversity within. The ethnic regionalization within the state of Jammu and Kashmir with a unitary kind of state structuration under the constitution of J&K with a complex of factors has estranged the people of Ladakh vis-a-vis the other two regions.

It is in this broader perspective that we have dealt with the case of Ladakh in the state of Jammu and Kashmir at micro-level. If India is a society comprising of a large number of diverse social, lingual, regional, religious or ethnic groups, the same pattern can be extended to the state of Jammu and Kashmir. If this diversity has hindered the process of nation-building at the national level, the state of J & K is also faced with the similar kind of problems in its efforts at state-building. The divergent forces within the state have failed to evolve a single consolidated view on the basis of which relations with India could be strengthened.

The Individuality of Ladakh

The current study shows that the long standing apparent regional variations and the divergence in the State of Jammu and Kashmir are not only geographical in content but also have ethno-cultural elements in operation. As regards the development of the sense of marginalisation among Ladakhis vis-a-vis Kashmir and Jammu, it is observed that since culture, language, religion and ethnicity play a significant role in the formation of group personality they tend to develop the sense of separate regional identity among Ladakhis.This becomes evident from the fact that Ladakh is culturally a homogeneous region strengthened by the reality that racially also they represent a distinct admixture of stock. This lends Ladakhis a distinctivity of their own and counterpoises them as distinct people against the other two regions which broadly represent different racial stocks and cultural backgrounds.

Language forms the most important medium of social interaction and communication in any area. It not only provides a platform for sharing common problems and concerns but also serves as an important vehicle of cultural progress. Under the prevalent circumstances the divisive role of language has also been witnessed by us in many states and regions and in the case of Ladakh also the role of language seems to have played a significant part.

In Ladakh, Ladakhi is spoken by about 40 percent of people followed by Balti (25 percent). Dardi, Tibetan and the Budhi are the other principal languages. However, the people of Ladakh (both Kargil and Leh) can understand and speak Hindi. Balti is more popular in Kargil district, whereas Ladakhi is widely spoken in the district of Leh. It has been observed that these languages of the region have sisterly characters and almost all the Ladakhis understand each other's dialects because of their shared origin.

The Ladakhi dialects with minor variations in the region of Ladakh is an important instrument of communication and social interaction. It serves as a substantial cohesive element to the society of Ladakh and has been the major instrument of public opinion in the region. Not only the religion (Buddhism), but more importantly the language forms the distinct Ladakhi culture and rich heritage that provides sustenance to the idea of Ladakhi oneness for mobilising the regional aspiration of having a vision of separate State or Union Territory.

With the grant of Scheduled Tribe status for the region as also Ladakh Autonomous Hill Development Council it is evident that the separate identity of the people of Ladakh has been officially recognised. The people of the region admitted the approval of the distinct Ladakhi identity (See Table No. 4.1) when asked during the survey.

The history of inter-regional tensions within the state of Jammu and Kashmir is well known since the days of Indian independence and Ladakh has registered its protest against the forced merger with J&K, both circumstantial and deliberate. Barring the acceptance of its demands for Scheduled Tribe status and Ladakh Autonomous Hill Development Council, a lot needs to be done from the standpoint of LBA and the newly formed Ladakh Union Territory Front (LUTF). In literacy, Ladakh has shown great progress as it has lagged behind the other two regions of Jammu and Kashmir. However, in respect of higher educational institutions till 2010, the region of Ladakh has only two Government Colleges and two Government Polytechnics (one each in Leh and Kargil) against a total of 204 colleges in Jammu and 131 colleges in Kashmir (These colleges include Government, Private, B. Ed., BCA, BBA, Law and Polytechnic colleges). The institutional imbalance is quite visible here that has been a great source of annoyance for Ladakhis.

In power sector the region has faced daunting task in the past. 18% respondents registered the non-availability of electricity in their areas. This is a matter of concern especially to people who have to face such hardships of nature. In the power sector the region has a bright future as many of the new projects in Ladakh are about to be completed in the next 5 to 8 years. This will not only meet the power requirements of the people but also increase the power revenue of the state corporation. In roads, health institutions, banks, landholdings and telecommunications (See Chapter 3) the region of Ladakh is better placed than the other regions since its small population makes it better served statistically.

However, the vast expanse of geography has its own limitations which deserve to be attended accordingly. Look of development, good capital inflow, lag in the industrial front, poor transportation, absence of all weather road connectivity, poor tourism and poor employment all add up to aggravate the regional feelings of Ladakh for a seperate state, union territory.

Ladakhis have been struggling for a dignified place in the constitutional set up of Jammu & Kashmir. Ladakhis, especially the Buddhists, have felt neglected and being accorded step-motherly treatment. Their educational, administrative, and economic aspirations are being deliberately ignored by the successive state governments. To counter such developments, Ladakhis have kept their pressure on both Centre and the state authorities which, in consequence, has strained the relations between the Kashmir and Ladakh regions.

Ladakh Buddhist Association (LBA) is the chief organisation that represents the popular grievances of the region. LBA is more of a cultural organization that aims at achieving the status of an Autonomous Hill Council for the region. It was way back in 1962 that Ladakhis first raised the demand for NEFA type administration. However, the rejection of their demand led them to look for greater regional autonomy in 1968. About four years later, they started agitating for UT status. Nevertheless, the LBA temporarily suspended its demand for Union Territory status in 1982 in view of some positive developments towards the formation of Autonomous Council and reverted back to the old demand for greater regional autonomy.

It was under these circumstances that President of India promulgated Constitutional (J&K) ST status orders on October 7, 1989 under Section A 341(1) of Indian Constitution. Through this order, Scheduled Tribe status was granted to eight communities — Balti, Beda, Bot, Bolo, Bropk, Dropka, Dard, Skin, Changpa, Corra, Mon and Puriyapa that covered 87.71 percent of the population of Leh and Kargil districts. It was a welcome development for Ladakhis as it opened the gates for some extra jobs and developmental opportunities. Asked about the grant of Scheduled Tribe status all respondents expressed happiness over it since it helps people in many ways i.e. more opportunities in education, jobs and allocation of more funds, hence more development.

The grant of Ladakh Autonomous Hill Development Councils to Leh and Kargil districts in 1995 and 2003 respectively is again a welcome step. 96% respondents have expressed happiness over the development. Ladakhis generally believe that the councils would be instrumental in meeting the various requirements of the region, community and people and lead to multifaceted development and better standard of life among the Ladakhis. However, the respondents showed unhappiness over the performance of the council. Only 48% respondents hold that the council has met the requirements of the people, while 40% respondents remained neutral and 12% disapproved the performance. Even about the devolution of sufficient powers to Ladakh Autonomous Hill Development Council, the respondents expressed unhappiness, as 30% of them deny the sufficient transfer of powers and 40% preferred to keep silent over the issue. Therefore, it is observed that devolution of more powers and revenue to Autonomous Councils are desirable and state government is advised to reconsider the devolution plan.

Since insurgency in the valley has caused anti-Indian feelings among the Kashmiris and they would accept nothing short of pre-1953 status (this has become a normal poll plank among political parties like NC and PDP, who participate in elections to the State Legislative Assembly and Indian Parliament) it has been observed that the other two regions of Ladakh and Jammu also have voiced their opinion against valley. Of course, the ethno-regional factors strengthen such reinforcing and when faced with strong economic hardships like lag in roads and communications, transport, educational institutions, hospitals, per capita income, development and flow of capital.

It has been established by the current study that the insurgency has caused in creating clefts in the bilateral relations between Leh and Kargil (See Table Nos. 5.6 & 5.7). Therefore, it is safe to argue that one of the prime reasons behind the divergence of the people of Ladakh vis-a-vis the other two regions especially Kashmir is insurgency that lands to insecurity and identity crisis in the region. A section of the respondents were of the view that insurgency has made inroads into the hearts of the people of Ladakh now and more peaceful the valley more stable the regions of the state. The Kargil episode is an example of this and people of the region are still alarmed over such kind of developments from across the borders. Theoretically too, it is believed that if a group which is in an advantageous position goes violent in a state, it tacitly reinforces the counter feelings in other people of the state, and divergence takes more acrid shape if such groups carry separate distinct identities.

The globalization that has reached the remotest of the corners of world, has influenced the society, culture and values of Ladakh also. Today people are more used to the luxuries that technology has offered and global market has reached at their door. With the rapid growth in literacy in the region people have become more conscious of the available opportunities in material and services. This changes the primordial assumptions and values of a community as people tend to look for the better ways of life. This seems to be true of the people of Ladakh also as the current study establishes that globalization has left deep impact on the socio-cultural life of the people of Ladakh.

The latest technology and the advent of modernizing forces like transport, communications and services that in turn facilitate the inflow of market forces, industry, and tourism etc. and upgradation in the living standards of people also affect the economy and ecology of a region. We have witnessed this in India. Global warming has caused melting of high mountains and glaciers in Himachal Pradesh, Jammu and Kashmir, Uttarakhand and Arunachal

Pradesh. This causes natural disasters and ecological imbalances in the region. The unexpected cloud burst and floods of Leh in August 2010 that destroyed property worth millions and took several lives might be one of the outcomes of this kind of development. The people of Ladakh feel highly scared of the phenomenon since it is first of its kind in the region for centuries and blame it on the construction, increased vehicular traffic and forestation by Indian forces as the cause behind it. The respondents agree that the process of modernization and globalization has left great impact on the environment of the region of Ladakh.

Globalization is being viewed as a process that has added to the existing divisions and rifts in people. With the break up of the stringent state controls and the free flow of goods, capital, investment, technology the world's becoming a battleground of the competing trans-national groups and multi-nationals, the ideas of protectionism and welfare have suffered adversely against the gigantism of market. In the current surge of events if the states are to witness immense increase in production and income the marginalized ones are to get further alienated and this is a matter of grave concern for the protagonists of the poor and the marginalized. It has been observed that not only in the developing world but even in the developed states the marginilisation of socially and economically poor people is taking place. The demands for the ouster of foreigners in U.S. and U.K. are just a symptomatic manifestation of the phenomenon.

Development has brought in its wake a host of its negatives too. If it leads to general uplift in life standards of people on the one hand it also cause conflicts. Development in a particular region can be a cause of concern for less developed regions, a phenomenon true of Jammu and Kashmir. The regions of Jammu and Ladakh have been raising the issue of discrimination by Valley for decades. As discussed in Chapter 4, the region of Ladakh feels deprived in the fields of educational institutions, health institutions, roads, tourism and many other areas. Even respondents would testify, though partially that the process of globalization/ modernization has added to the sift among different regions i.e. Jammu, Kashmir and Ladakh.

The reference here is towards the development and governance side where the region of Ladakh feels estranged because of neglect. Closely associated with it is the question of cultural identity of the people. The Ladakhis, as is true of most of the tribes in India, feel that the modernizing and globalizing forces are weakening the cultural fabric and old customs and traditions in favour of consumerism and luxuries that market offers. The current study establishes that Ladakhis strongly affirm the view that the process of globalization / modernization has endangered the separate identity of the people of Ladakh and it requires to be protected, of course the way Ladakhis would suggest i.e. by grant of Union Territory or separate statehood status to them.

The idea of an independent unit within a federal set up may appeal to every people and it is no wonder if the people of a region like Ladakh look for the same. Autonomy itself is a substitute for development since it is believed that in a self-governed region people have systems of checks and balances and they go for faster development than centrally-governed units. The idea of Union Territory may fall short of these aspirations but this seems to be a step towards real autonomous status within the constitutional set up of India very much in line with the rest of the Indian states.

While pondering about the future status of the region, the current study establishes that a vast majority of them want segregation of the region from the state of Jammu and Kashmir (though a small number of respondents mostly Kargilites are against the option). This seems to be the unfinished agenda of most of the Ladakhis to have an independent status outside the ambit of Jammu and Kashmir.

The people of the region are curious about this and they want to continue with the long standing demand of LBA, though at times withdrawn, for the segregation of the region from Jammu and Kashmir and creation of a new state or Union Territory. This is another thing that under the power equations and complexity of Kashmir problem the idea of trifurcation of Jammu & Kashmir is considered dangerous with dire consequences. However, taken into account how the valley has behaved over the decades it seems to be imprudent to forcibly keep the other two regions bound with it. On the other hand the trifurcation is expected to trigger a new development related activities in the other two regions.

Recommendations

Apparently, the State of Jammu and Kashmir has long standing regional variations and divergences which are not only geographical but ethno-cultural too. Ladakh as a region has a distinct identity of its own and its community which is characterised by separate language, culture, religion and ethnicity marks it entirely different from the rest of the people of State. It provides a substantial cohesive element to the society of Ladakh and has been the major platform for mobilization of public opinion in the region. It is not only the religion and racial distinctivity, but, more importantly the language that shapes the distinct Ladakhi culture and rich heritage that provides sustenance to the idea of Ladakhi oneness, and the regional aspiration of having a vision of separate State or Union Territory.

This has been the finding of the current study which reveals that in respect of higher educational institutions till 2011, the region of Ladakh has only two Government Colleges and two Government Polytechnics (one each in Leh and Kargil) as against a total of 204 colleges in Jammu and 131 colleges in Kashmir which shows that there is a huge institutional imbalance that provides a potential issue of annoyance for Ladakhis. Hence, it is recommended, that the state government should look into the disparity and open more such institutions in the region.

In power sector, the region faced a daunting task in the past. 18% respondents registered the non-availability of electricity in their areas. This is a matter of grave concern especially to people who have to face such hardships. Although, there are many projects on the way, yet, the state government can go for better alternative of power (non-conventional sources like solar energy, wind mills etc.) as makeshift arrangements, since laying of line to the remote and distant areas can turn out to be a difficult job at times.

The present study finds that in the case of roads, health institutions, banks, landholdings and telecommunications the region of Ladakh is better placed than the other regions since its small population makes it better served statistically. However, the vast expanse of geography has its own limitations which deserve to be attended to accordingly. Even the respondents' view over the non-availability of doctors and free medicines in hospitals and non-availability of teachers in schools (though the absence of these services is small in percentage) make the things difficult for the people. What, if people are not getting drinking water, the basic amenity of life. Therefore it is desired that the government should do the needful to ensure these basic services.

The absence of good capital inflow, lag in the industrial

front, poor transportation, lack of all weather road connectivity, poor tourism and unemployment all mess up the things. It is recommended that the roads, the real veins of the flow of capital and march towards development, should be extended to cover almost all the corners of the region however difficult the terrains may be. The high altitudes of passes and mountains that hinder the flow of vehicles to Srinagar and Manali for about six months should be traversed. Tunnelling seems to be the only way out to an area that lies to the south-west of formidable China which has turned the whole of Tibet into a web of roads, railways and airstrips. Even from defence perspective, this area needs special attention since the theory of invincibility of vast barren deserts and dry mountains by a strong enemy carries little weight now. Most of the Ladakhi respondents have also suggested the building of strong infrastructural facilities and defence against Chinese movement over the borders. The Chinese defence budget is three times than that of India and Government of India shouldn't hesitate in building strong infrastructure at least along the border areas.

The grant of Ladakh Autonomous Hill Development Councils to Leh and Kargil districts in 1995 and 2003 respectively was a welcome step since Ladakhis believe that the councils shall be instrumental in meeting the various requirements of the region, and lead to multifaceted development and better standard of life among Ladakhis. However, the current study establishes that Ladakhis are unhappy over the performance of the councils. The powers mentioned in the Act may look abundant but the actual exercise of these powers by Ladakh Autonomous Hill Development Councils makes it clear that a lot needs to be done since whatever they have got is administered and managed politically. "Councils don't enjoy sufficient powers" lament the Ladakhis. Therefore, it is observed that more devolution of powers and revenue heads towards Autonomous Councils are desirable and state Government is advised to reconsider the devolution plan.

Insurgency in the region of Kashmir has also influenced the other two regions of Ladakh and Jammu. Of course, the ethno-regional factors stengthen counter reinforcing and when compounded by strong economic components like lag in roads and communications, transport, educational institutions, hospitals, per capita income, development and flow of capital, the situation turns worse. It has been established by the current study that the phenomenon of insurgency has helped creating fissures in the bilateral relations between Leh and Kargil. Insurgency has its inroads into the hearts of the people of Ladakh now and more peaceful the valley more stable the regions of the state. The Kargil episode represents the worst of this and people of the region are still alarmed over such kind of developments from across the borders. Therefore, if the region looks for segregation it is duly justified since peace and security of life is the right of every peace loving people.

The process of globalization that permeates to the remotest of the corners of world has influenced the society, culture and values of Ladakh. This changes the primordial assumptions and values of a community as people tend to look for the better ways of life. The flow of technology and the advent of modernizing forces like transport, communications and services that in turn facilitate the inflow of market forces, industry, and tourism etc. and upgrade the living standards of people also affect the geo-spatiality and ecology of a region. This is the hard reality of our times that in India global warming has caused melting of high mountains and glaciers in Himachal Pradesh,

Jammu and Kashmir, Uttarakhand and Arunachal Pradesh. We are witness to severe ecological and natural disasters. The unexpected cloud burst and floods of Leh in August 2010 that destroyed property worth millions and took several lives might be one of the outcomes of this kind of development.

Forestation is not a phenomenon causative of excess of nature's wrath rather it brings more energy and fluidity in life of people. It provides wood for fuel and construction, relief from scorching sun as also fodder for animals. The area needs to be protected from the traffic menace and unruly tourists as also from too much gaseous emission for which stringent penalties can be fixed. Of course this can be done only in collaboration with other states. Himachal has set an example by prohibiting polythene and smoking in public places. The same can be followed in J&K.

Development has its negatives too. If on the one hand it leads to general uplift in life standards of people it is also causative of interest consciousness and consequently conflicts. Development in a particular region can be a cause of concern for relatively less developed regions, a phenomenon true of Jammu and Kashmir. The Ladakhis, as is true of most of the tribes in India, feel that the modernizing and globalizing forces are weakening the cultural fabric and old customs and traditions in favour of consumerism and luxuries that market offers. The current study establishes that Ladakhis strongly affirm the view that the process of globalization/modernization has endangered the separate identity of the people of Ladakh and it requires to be protected, of course the Ladakhis would suggest i.e. grant of Union territory or separate statehood status to them.

Since Ladakh is culturally a homogeneous region with a

distinctivity of its own against the other two regions which broadly represent different ethnic stocks and cultural backgrounds, the Ladakhi quest requires to be seriously understood. It is another thing that under the given power equations and complexity of Kashmir problem the idea of trifurcation of Jammu & Kashmir is considered to be fraught with adverse consequences. However, taken into account how the valley has behaved over the decades it seems to be imprudent to forcibly keep the other two regions bound with it. On the other, the trifurcation is bound to trigger a new vigour into the development related activities of the other two regions.

Bibliography

Primary Sources

Section I

Field Survey, 2011, (Area- Region of Ladakh), Project: ***Inter-regional Divergence in Jammu and Kashmir: A Study of Ladakh Region.***

Section II

Census Atlas, 1981.

Census of India, 1971.

Census of India, 2011.

Constitution of India.

Constitution of Jammu and Kashmir.

Digest of Statistics 2001-02, Government of J & K: Directorate of Economics & Statistics, Planning & Development, 2003.

Districts of Jammu and Kashmir, 2009, Directorate of Economics and Statistics, 2010, Jammu and Kashmir, 2010.

Economic Review of J & K 1990, Directorate of Economics and Statistics, Jammu and Kashmir. 1990.

Economic Review of J & K 1989, Directorate of Economics and Statistics, Jammu and Kashmir, 1990.

Eighth & Five Year Plan 1992-97, Vol. II, Government of India, Planning Commission, N. Delhi, 1998.

First International Ladakh Workshop, Germany, 1981.

Gazetteer of Kashmir and Ladakh, New Delhi, Vivek Publishing House, 1890/1974.

http://censusindia.gov.in/2011-prov-results/prov_ data_ products_J&K.html

http://www. http://jkspdc.nic.in/

Indian Economic Diary, 1986.

Indian Economic Diary. 1987.

Indian Economic Diary, 1992.

Indicators of Regional Development : 1985-86., Govt. of J & K, Directorate of Economics & Statistics, Planning & Dev., 1987.

Irrigation Statistics: 1950-51 to 1985-86, Government of J & K: Directorate of Economics & Statistics, Planning & Development, 1987.

Jammu and Kashmir in Indian Economy, Directorate of Economics & Statistics, Planning & Development Department, 1990.

Performance Review of Jammu and Kashmir 2008-09, Directorate of Economics and Statistics, Jammu and Kashmir. 2010.

Socio-Economic Profile of Jammu and Kashmir-2009, Directorate of Economics and Statistics, J&K, 2009.

Socio-Economic Profile of Jammu and Kashmir-2010, Directorate of Economics and Statistics, J&K, 2010.

SIRI Directory of Industries of India, Delhi : Small Industries Research Institute, 1991.

The Ladakh Autonomous Hill Development Councils Act of 1995, Gazette of India, May 9, 1995.

The Times of India Directory & Year Book 1984, Bombay The Times of India Press, 1985.

Secondary Sources

Books

Bamzai, P.N.K., *A History of Kashmir: Political, Social and Cultural,* New Delhi: Metropolitian Books Co., 1962.

Cunningham, Alexander, *Ladakh: Physical, Statistical and Historical,* Delhi: 1972.

Diwan, Pervez, *Jammu, Kashmir and Ladakh,* New Delhi: Manas Publications, 2008.

Drew, Frederick, *Jammu & Kashmir Territories,* New Delhi: Cosmo Publications, 1976.

Driessen, H. and Otto, T. (eds), *Perplexities of Identification: Anthropological Studies in Cultural Differentiation and the Use of Resources.* Aarhus: University Press, 2000.

Francke, A. H., *A History of Ladakh,* New Delhi: Sterling Publishers, 1977.

Francke, A. H., *Ladakh: The Mysterious Land,* New Delhi: Ess Ess Publications, 1980.

Ganhar, J.N. and Ganhar, P.N., *Budhism in Kashmir and Ladakh,* New Delhi, 1956.

Hussain, Majid, "Tourism in the Suru Valley: Prospects and Problems", in S.C. Singh, (Ed.), *Impact of Tourism on Mountain Environment,* Meerut: Research India Publications, 1989.

Jagmohan, *My Frozen Turbulence in Kashmir,* New Delhi: Allied Publishers, 1991.

Jina, P.S. and Zain-ul-Abeidin, *Islam in Kashmir,* New Delhi: Atlantic, 2007.

Jina, Prem Singh, *Ladakh: Land and People,* New Delhi: Indus publishing Company, 1996.

Kapur, M.C., *Kingdom of Kashmir,* Jammu: Kashmir History Publishers, 1984.

Kaul, S. & Kaul, H. N., *Ladakh Through the Ages, Towards a New Identity,* Nataraj Books, Springfield, VA, 1992.

Lamb, Alstair, *Kashmir: A Disputed Legacy, 1946-1990,* Karachi: Oxford University Press, 1992,

Lambert, Cowley, *Trip to Cashmer and Ladakh,* London: 1877.

Lawrence, Walter, *The Valley of Kashmir,* Delhi: Asian Educational services, 1887.

Moorcraft, William and Trebek, George, *Travels in the Himalayan Provinces of Hindustan and the Punjab, In Ladakh and Kashmir, in Peshawar, Kabul, Kunduz and Bokhara,* London, 1837.

Om, Hari, Chaudhary, Rekha and Sharma, R.D., *Politics of Autonomy in Jammu and Kashmir,* Jammu: Vinod Publishers, 1999.

Pallis, Marco, *Peaks and Lamas,* London: Cassel and Company Ltd., 1939.

Parmu, R.K., *History of Muslim Rule in Kashmir-1320 to 1819,* New Delhi: People's Publishing House, 1969.

Puri, Balraj, *Simmering Volcano: A Study in Jammu's Relations with Kashmir,* New Delhi: Sterling Publishers, 1983.

Puri, Balraj, *Triumph and Tragedy of Indian Federalization,* New Delhi: Sterling Publishers, 1983.

Ram, Hari, *Special Status in Indian Constitution: Jammu & Kashmir,* New Delhi: Seema Publications, 1983.

Ray, S.C., *Early History and Culture of Kashmir,* Delhi: 1970.

Rizvi, Janet, *Ladakh: Crossroads of High Asia.* Delhi: Oxford University Press, 1999.

Rizvi, Janet, *Trans-Himalayan Caravans: Merchant Princes and Peasant Traders in Ladakh.* Delhi: Oxford University Press, 2000.

Shakspo, N. T., *A Cultural History of Ladakh,* Edited by Kyle Gardener, Leh: Centre for Research on Ladakh, 2005.

Sharma, B.L., *Kashmir Awakes,* New Delhi: Vikas Publishing House, 1971.

Snellgrove, D.L. and Skorupski, T., *The Cultural Heritage of Ladakh,* Vol. I, Delhi, 1977.

Srinivas, S., *The Mouths of People, the Voice of God,* Oxford Univ. Press, New York, 1998.

Stein, M.A., *Rajatarangini,* (rendered into English), Vol. I&II, London: Constable, 1907.

Stein, R.A., *Tibetan Civilization,* London, 1972.

Sunita, *Politics of State Autonomy and Regionalism,* Kalpaz, New Delhi, 2007.

Thakur, Harish K., *Alienation and Integration in Jammu and Kashmir,* Jaipur: Alekh Publishers, 1999.

Thomas Watters, *On Yuan Chwang's Travels in India, 629-645 AD,* Vol. I.

Thubstan, Paldan, *A Brief Guide to the Buddhist Monasteries and Royal Castles of Ladakh,* 1976.

Tokan, Sumi D., Oki, Masato and Hassnain, Fida M., *Ladakh the Moonland,* New Delhi: Light and Life Pub. Co.,1975.

Zain-ul-Abeidin, *Emergence of Islam in Ladakh,* New Delhi: Atlantic Publishers, 2009.

Papers and Articles

Beek, Martijn van, "Dissimulations: Representing Ladakhi Identity", in H. Driessen and T. Otto (eds), *Perplexities of Identification: Anthropological Studies in Cultural Differentiation and the Use of Resources.* Aarhus: University Press, 2000.

Beek, Martijn Van, "Hill Councils, Development and Democracy: Assumptions and Experiences from Ladakh", *Alternatives,* 2000.

Beek, Martijn van, "Hill Councils, Development, and Democracy: Assumptions and Experiences from Ladakh", *Alternatives: Global, Local, Political,* Vol. 24, No. 4, Oct.-Dec. 1999.

Beek, Martijn van, "Imaginaries of Ladakhi Modernity", in Barnett, R., Schwartz, R. (eds), *Tibetan Modernities: Notes from the Field on Cultural and Social Change.*

Beek, Martijn van, "The Importance of Being Tribal, Or The Impossibility of Being Ladakhis", in T. Dodin and H. Rather (eds), *Recent Research on Ladakh.*

Ulm: Ulmi University, 1999.

Beek, Martijn van, "Lessons from Ladakh? Local Responses to Globalization and Social Change". 2008.

Bhatt, R.K., "Jammu & Kashmir", in Iqbal Narain, (Ed.), *State Politics in India,* Meerut: Meenakshi Prakashan, 1976

Bose, T., Mohan, D., G. Navlakha and S. Banerjee, "India's Kashmir War", *Economic and Political Weekly,* March 31, 1990.

Federations, Vol. 3, No. 2 , May 2003.

Fisher, Margret W., "Ladakh and the Sino-Indian Border Crisis", *Asian Survey,* Vol. 2, No. 8 (Oct., 1962

Ghosh, D.N., "Kashmir and India", *Economic and Political Weekly,* Vol. XXVI , No. 34, August 24, 1991,

Irshad A. Navchoo and G. M. Buth, "Ethnobotany of Ladakh, India: Beverages, Narcotics", *Economic Botany,* Vol. 44, No. 3, Jul. - Sep. 1990.

Jain , R.B., "Political System and Nation Building : The Indian Political Experience", in S.A.H. Haqqi, (Ed.), *Democracy, Pluralism and nation-Building,* N.Delhi :N.B.O. Publishers, 1984,

Kothari, Rajni, *Politics in India,* New Delhi: Orient Longman, 1972.

Krais & Hoffman, Martijin van Beek, *Identity Fetishism, and the Art of Representation, the long struggle for regional autonomy in Ladakh.* A Ph.D. thesis submitted to Cornell University.

Kumar, Ravinder, "Anguish of Kashmiris: An Agenda for Countering Alienation" , *The Times of India,* May, 1992.

Leiden, Brill, Martijin van Beek, 2007, "After Autonomy: Development and Politics in Ladakh", *Trin-gyi-pho-nya,* Vol. 5, 2008.

Mcgarry, John, *"Can Federalism Help to Manage Ethnic and National Diversity"*?

Puri , Balraj, "Challenge in Kashmir", *Economic and Political Weekly,* Vol XXV, No 4, January 27, 1990,

Puri, Balraj, Route of Ladakh's Integration, Economic and Political Weekly, Vol. 17, No. 8, 1982.

Thomas, F. W., "Tibetan Documents concerning Chinese Turkestan. I: The Ha-za", *Journal of the Royal Asiatic Society of Great Britain and Ireland,* No. 1, Jan., 1927.

Tikku, M.K., "Kashmir Today III, Economy remains Unaffected ", *The Hindustan Times,* October 2, 1992.

Tikku, M.K., "NC Stumbling Block to Hill Council", *The Hindustan Times,* October 5, 1992.

Vinaik, Achin, " Overplaying Balkanization Dragon to India", *Indian Express,* October 5, 1992.

Wirth, T., Wang, Xiaoyan, Linz, Bodo, et.al., "Distinguishing Human Ethnic Groups by Means of Sequences from Helicobacter pylori: Lessons from" , *Proceedings of the National Academy of Sciences of the United States of America,* Vol. 101, No. 14, Apr. 6, 2004.

Index

Accession to India, 53
Administrative and
  Economic Level, 162, 166
  Political Structure, 21
Advantaged Groups, 160
Afghan Territory of Wakhan, 11
Agricultural Labour, 76, 79
Agriculture, Largest Occupation, 81
Air Strips in Tibet, 148
Alchi Monastery, 33
Ali Mir; Balti Ruler, 37
Alluvial fans, 24
Amarnath Shrine, Kashmir, 108
Ambedkar, Dr. BR, 52
American Model, 48
Anantnag, 66
  Kargil and Kupwara, 101
Ancient
  Civilization, 26
  Times Kashmir, 33
    A Centre of Buddhism, 33

Anti-Valley Feelings, 10
Article-370 of Indian Constitution, 47, 51, 55, 105, 178, 180, 181
Ashoka, 33
Asia
  And Africa, 48
  Africa & Latin American States, 203
Asian Tribes, 26
Assembly Units- HMT, ITI, 104
Aurangzeb, Mughal Emperor, 40
Autonomous
  Council, 190, 217
  Hill Council, 59, 209
Awami National Conference (ANC), 57

Baghlihar Power Project, 83
Balti (s), 28, 32, 67
Baltistan (Pakistan Occupied Kashmir), 35, 37
Bangladesh, 120
Banking Facility, 156
Banks, 156, 208, 215
  In Jammu and Kashmir, 100
  Of River Indus, 23
  Of Zanskar River, 25
Bar Association, 57
Baramulla, 66
Baribrahaman Industrial Complex in Jammu, 103
Barrenness of Ladakh, 105
Bazo Mosque, 37
Beda, 30
Belgium, 49, 120
Bharatiya Janata Party (BJP), 57, 61
Bi-Annual Movement of Durbar, 58
Bogdang Masjid, 37
Border
  Area Development Program, 60
  Conflict, Between India and China, 9

British
  India, 11
  North American Act, 1867, 52
Brutal Police Repression, 60
Budhi Language, 67
Buddhism, 28, 29, 33, 34, 35
  And Aryan and Tibetan Culture, 28
  Egalitarian Structure, 29
Buddhist (s), 64, 65, 81, 177
  And Muslim Communities, 30
  Clergy, 35
  Culture, 59
  Dominated Leh, 59
  Majority Area of Ladakh, 13
  Majority Ladakh, 62
  Missionaries of Ashoka, 33
  Monks of Ladakh, 28
  Of Ladakh, 60
  Teaching Centres, 34

Canada, 49
Carpet Weaving, 157
Caucasoid (Aryan) Blood, 28
Ceasefire Agreement (Jan-1, 1949), 11
Central
  Asia, 21
  Asian Trade, 38
  Tibet, 28
Chang Thang Sub Division, 22, 26, 31
Chattergal as Dowry, Area beyond, 36
Chemical Fertilizers, 90
Child Birth, A Social Event, 31
China, 21, 22, 97, 148, 200, 216
  Occupied Kashmir, 40
  Occupied Tibet, 1950, 35
  Railway Line upto Lhasa, 148
Chinese
  Defence Budget, 216
  Incursions, 29
  Movement Over Borders, 201, 216
Chomos, Female Lama, 29, 30
Chushot
  Gongma, 37
  Yokma, 37
Chutak HEP, 87
Class Structure, 119
Clay Moulding, 157
Colonial Powers, 49
Colonialism, 203
Communist States, 48
  Czechoslovakia, 48
  Nigeria, 48
  USSR, 48
  Yugoslavia, 48
Communities, 61
  Balti, 61
  Beda, 61
  Bolo, 61
  Bot, 61
  Bropk, 61
  Changpa, 61
  Corra, 61
  Dard, 61
  Mon, 61
  Puriyapa, 61
  Skin, 61
Community-wise Employment, 81
Conflicts and Armed Struggles, 50
Congress (I), 51
Constituent Assembly, 52, 53, 54
Constitution
  drafting committee, 52
  (J&K) ST Status Orders, 60, 209
  Of India, 32, 43, 44, 51, 55, 178
  Of Jammu and Kashmir, 41, 44, 178, 182, 205
Corruption, 82
Cross Border Terrorism, 10
Cultivation, 23
Cultural
  Disparities, 159
  Identity, 9, 10, 201
  Values and Traditions, 130

Dah SHP—Pugah Geothermal Project, 87
Dardi Language, 67
Dardistan, 27
Dards, 27, 44
Death Ceremony (Sheston), 32
Decentralization of Powers, 51
Development
  Of Industry, 157
  Projects, 103
    Bandipore, 103
    Bhaderwah, 103

Leh, 193
Pampore, 103
Rajouri, 103
Samba, 103
Udhampur, 103
Devolution of Powers, 217
DIC (District Industry Centres), 103, 157
Diksit, 37
Directorate of Economics and Statistics, J&K, 80
Disadvantaged Groups, 160
District Blocks, 19
Chuchot, 19
Durbuk, 19
Khaltsi, 19
Kharu, 19
Leh, 19
Nubra, 19
Nyoma, 19
Panamic, 19
Saspol, 19
District
Budgam, 66, 70
Doda, Poonch and Rajouri, 65, 101
Jammu and Kathua, 70, 101, 105
Kargil, 18, 19, 20, 21, 22, 43, 61, 65, 67, 72,169, 216
Ladakh and Kargil, 96
Leh, 20, 21, 22, 26, 32, 39-41, 43, 61, 65, 67
Mirpur, 11
Muzzafarabad, 11
Pulwama, 66
Riasi, 58
Srinagar, 22, 66,101, 102
Srinagar, Baramula, Anantnag 22
Udhampur, Kathua and Jammu, 65
Districts in Jammu Region, 56
Bandipore, 56
Kishtwar, 56
Riasi, 56, 58
Samba, 56
District-Wise Population, 12, 13
Dmang-Rigs, 29
Doctors and Nurses in Hospitals, 145
Doda, Kathua, Srinagar Districts, 101
Dogra, Girdhari Lal, MP, 57
Dominion of
India, 53
Pakistan, 53
Domkhar Hydel Project, 60
Drass, 44
And Lamayuru, 27
And Nimu, 27
And Wakha Chu, 19
And Zanskar, 34
Valley, 23
Drinkable Water, 152, 158
Dulhasti, 83
Durbar Issue, 58, 61

East of Iran, 22
Eastern Europe, 48
Ecological Imbalances, 212
Economic
And Political Powers, 190
Development, 15, 102, 111, 188
Opportunities, 159
Policies, 60
Economy, 89, 119, 156
Education, 140
Educational
And Medical Institutions, 158
Institutions, 72, 73, 74
Elections, 191
Participation, 193
Electricity, 153, 158
Embroidery, 157
Essential Commodities, 147
Ethiopia, 49
Ethnic
And Communal Groups, 48
And Religious Groups, 49
Groups, 50
Linguistics Division, 49
Nationalism, 205
Tensions, 50

Farooq Abdullah's Government, 56
Farooq's National Conference, 57
Federal
Structure, 50, 51
System, 186
Federalism, 48, 204
Festivals and Ceremonies, 30
Financial Powers, 180

Five Rivers, 11
Chenab, 11
Jhelum, 11
Ravi, 11
Satluj, 11
Five Year Plans 83, 108, 109
Floods of Leh, 133, 212
Forestry, 79
Fotu La Pass, 22
Fourth Legendary Council, 34
Free Medicines in Hospitals, 146, 215
French, 48
And English Education Rights, 49
Fruit
Growers, 60
Processing, 157
Fundamental Rights, 50
Fundamentalism, 10
Fundamentalist Missionaries, 63

Gandhi, Indira, 107
Gedun, Buddhist who Undertake Celibacy as Lifetime Vow, 29
Geographical Barriers, 143
Germany, 120
Gilgit, 11, 22
Gilgit-Baltistan, (Pakistan Occupied Kashmir), 19
Glaciers in-, 133
Arunachal Pradesh, 133
Himachal Pradesh, 133, 211, 217
Jammu and Kashmir, 133
Uttarakhand, 133
Global Warming, 211
Globalization, 15, 17, 124, 128, 130, 132, 205, 211, 212, 217
Impact on Socio-Economic, Political, Cultural Life, 16, 17
Gold Granite dust District, 23
Gompa, 41
Gompa of Alchi, 40
Gongma, 37
Good Infrastructure, 157
Communication, 157
Electricity, 157
National Resources, 157
Railways, 157
Governance, 47, 48; 51, 159, 188
Government of India Act 1935, 50
Governor General of India, 53
Grants and Development Funds, 165
Graves of-, 36
Chosbum Ldey, 36
Mosolu Begum, 36
Rgyalbum Ldey, 36
Great
Britain, 11
Himalayas, 21
Gulmantango Pastures, 25
Gupta, Janakraj, MP, 57
Gyal Khatun, 37

Halqa Panchayats, 193
Handicraft Industries, 111
Handicrafts, 157
Handloom (s), 157
Silk Weaving Factory Rambagh, 103
Weaving Factory Shirinbagh, 103
Health
Hazards, 144
Institutions, 99, 208, 215
Hemis, 41
Hiuen Tsang, 27
Higher Education, 142
Hill
Area Development Project, 103
Development Council, 186, 188
Himachal Pradesh, 18, 22, 165
And Punjab, 82
Himalayan Mountain Ranges, 23
Kunlun, 23
The Ladakh, 23
The Muztagh, 23
Zanskar, 23
Himalayan Range, 22, 25
Hindu
Majority Jammu, 13
Organizations in Jammu and Ladakh, 63
Second Largest Community, 64
Hindus, 81
Hospitals And
Dispensaries, 143, 145
Free Medicines, 146
House Boats, 106
Hunder Mosque, 37

Hydro-Electric Power, 153

IAS
  Officers, 81
  Services, 81
Identity Crisis, 172
Id-ul-Gadeer, 37
Igoo, The Irrigation Projects, 60
Image of Mahakal, 41
Imam Barahs, 37
  Chushot Yokma, 37
Imam Barahs in Leh, 37
Imamia Jama Masjid Leh, 37
Import and Export of Essential Commodities, 147
Important Fruits of State, 93
  Apple—Mango, 93
Independent Political Identity, 176
India, 21, 49, 120
  And China, 9
  And Pakistan, 11
  Ethno-Federalism, 49
  World's Largest Democracy, 49
Indian
  Constitution, 51, 52, 54, 55, 204
  Federal System, 204
  Federation, 47, 52
  Forces, 133, 212
  Independence Act, 1947, 53
  Railways, 106
  Society, 204
  States, 53
  Union, 53
Individuality of Ladakh, 206
Indo-
  Bulgarian Project, 93
  Pakistan and Indo-Sino Border, 60
Indus Valley, 23, 24, 26, 27
Industrial and Democratic Revolutions, 203
Industrialization, 102, 111, 203
Industry (ies), 153, 157
Information Technology Revolution, 124
Inscriptions of Buddhism, 33
Insecurity and Identity Crisis, 211
Instrument of Accession, 53, 54
Insurgency, 18, 171, 172, 174, 201
International
  Brotherhood and National Integration, 106
  Democratic Front of Youth Organization, 57
Inter-Regional
  Divergence, 119-158, 159-201
    Ladakh Phase I, 119-158
    Ladakh-II, 159-201
  Diversity, 10
  Tensions, 56, 207
Intra-Regional
  Roads, 147
  Tensions, 15
Iranian Revolution, 62
Iran-Iraq War, 107
Iraq, 48
ISI, 10
Islam, 35, 36, 37, 64
Islamic
  Communities, 63
  Culture, 62
  Fundamentalism, 63
  Militancy, 62
  Polity, 59

Jagmohan, Governor, 83
Jamaat-i-Islami, 10
Jamaat-run Institutions, 63
Jama Masjid, Leh 40
Jammu, 37
  Based Dogras, 14
  Card, 61
  Region, (Kishtwar, Ramban, or Doda), 12, 79, 91, 92, 94, 103
    Jammu, Kathua, Punch, Rajauri, Udhampur, Reasi, Samba,), 12
Jammu and Kashmir (J&K), 9-11, 13, 22, 47-117, 120, 136, 153, 167, 196, 199, 205-208, 214
  And Himachal Pradesh, 31
  Handicrafts Corporation, 103
  Hydro Electric Projects Development Policies, 2014, 88
  Industries, 102
  Inter-Regional Divergence in-, 47-117
  Minerals, 102
  Region, 70

Religion Wise Population, 14
State Power Development Corporation, JKSPDC), 84
Strategically Important Area, 11
Jammuites And Ladakhis, 62
Janata Party, 57
Jehadis of the Valley, 14
Jina, 26
Jing-sReg Ceremony, 32
Joint Action Committee, 57
Judiciary, 51

Kailash Range, 24
Kanishwal Project,Kanihama, 103
Karakoram Range, 19, 22, 23, 24
Kargil, 38, 65
And Leh, 142
Autonomous Hill Council, 176
Borders of Pakistan, 43
District Blocks, 19
Drass, 19
GM Pore/Trespone, 19
Kargil, 19
Lungnak, 19
Sankoo, 19
Shakra-Chitkan, 19
Shargol, 19
Taisuru, 19
Zanskar, 19
District Composite Culture, 44
Balti—Shia Culture, 44
District Sub-Divisions, 43
Episode, 211
Muslim Majority Area, 20, 167
Region, 177
Town, 22
Kargilite, 214
Muslims, 199
Karsha in Zanskar, 41
Kartse Khar, Sculptures of Bodhi Sattava Maitreya, 34
Kashmir, 13, 14, 27, 34, 34, 35, 36, 36, 60, 63, 71, 79, 103, 109, 110, 204, 210
And Ladakh Regions, 61, 208
And Yarkand, 34
Card, 61
Handicrafts, 103
Problem, 214, 219
Province, 11
Physiography of-, 11
Region (Anantnag, Pulwama, Srinagar, Badgam, Baramullah, Kupwara, Kulgam, Bandipore, Ganderbal and Shupian Districts), 12, 65, 72, 75, 79, 92, 94, 99
Kashmiri
Language, 66
Leaders, 61
Muslims, 81
Painters, 34
Kashmiris, 14, 55, 56, 63, 210
Khachay Masjid of Mulbek, 36
Oldest Mosque of Ladakh Region, 36
Kha-La-Che, 27
Khan, MY, Jammu and Kashmir Tourism, 107
Khanqah, 37
King
Jam Yang Naamgyal, 37
Kanishka, 34
Langdarma, 28
Kingdom of Kanishka, 34
Kishanganga, 83
Kishtwar, 58
and Kargil, 45
Ko-hu-lo, 27
Kullu and Lahul, 27
Kupwara, 66, 70
Kushak Bakula's LBA, 58, 176

Ladakh, 59, 60, 66, 67, 71, 72, 75, 76, 80, 103
Kargil and Leh Districts, 12
Tribal Status, 15
And Baltistan, 32, 36
And Jammu, 10, 72
And Kargil Region, 89
And Kashmir, 80
And Kashmir Region, 91
Autonomous Hill Council, (LAHC), 15, 17
Autonomous Hill Development Council (LAHDC), 16, 41, 44, 160, 186, 188, 190, 193, 207, 209, 210, 216

- Bar Association, 60, 207, 209
- Buddhist Association (LBA), 14, 58, 59, 176
  - Movement, 65
- Buddhist Majority Region, 171
- Culture and Values, 132
- Dynasty, 35
- For a Separate State, 208
- Mountain Passes in-, 25, 26
- Physiography, 22
- Political Autonomy, 15
- Region, 65, 79, 82, 99
- Society, Religion and Economy, 28
- Sparsely Populated Region of India, 9
- Sub-Regional Identity, 10
- Vis-à-vis Jammu and Kashmir, 160
  - Relations of-, 15
- Where Earth and Sky Meet, 23

Ladakhi, 208, 209
- Culture, 207
- Dialects, 207
- Geo-Spatial Reality, 30
- Identity, 16, 17, 207
- Language, 32, 206
- Leaders, 57
- Union Territory Front (LUTF), 15, 207

Ladakhis, 9, 14, 15, 17, 18, 31, 36, 56, 59, 60, 61, 65, 67, 75, 108, 124, 126, 158, 160, 162, 163, 198, 200, 201, 206, 209, 210, 213, 214, 216, 217, 218
- And Kashmiri, 82
- Vis-à-vis Kashmir and Jammu, 14
- Vis-à-vis Kashmir and Ladakh, 65

LADC Act, 41, 44

Lahul
- And Spiti (Himachal Pradesh), 35, 40
- Spiti Area, 18, 19

Lalitaditya, Famous King from Kashmir, 35

Lamas, 29, 31, 32, 33
- Also Act As Medical Practitioner, 32

Lamayuru, 41

Landholdings, 91

Lang Dar Ma, Tibetan King, 35

Languages, 66, 206
- Balti, 206
- Budhi, 206
- Dardi, 206
- Dogri, 66
- Gojri, 66
- Hindi, 206
- Kashmiri, 66
- Ladakhi, 66, 206
- Pandi, 66
- Punjabi, 66
- Tibetan, 206
- Urdu, 66

La-rtsa, 28

Lashkar-e-Taiyyiba, 10

Law and Order, 102

Legislative Assembly, 59

Leh, 22, 37, 41, 65, 72, 186, 200
- And Kargil, 18, 39, 59, 70, 71, 97, 207, 210, 217
- And Kashmir, 19
- Blocks, 41
- Buddhist Majority District, 20
- Buddhists, 169
- Palace (Seven Storeyed), 40
- Sub-Divisions, 41
  - Chang Thang, 41
  - Khaltsi, 41
  - Nubra, 41

Length of Roads, 148

Lhasa, 35, 97

Life Expectancy, 143-144

Likir Monastery, 40

Literacy, 58-70, 82
- Female, 68
- Growth in-, 140
- In Jammu and Kashmir, 68
- In Ladakh, 75
- Male, 68
- Rate, 70, 71

Livestock, 38, 79

Living Standards of People, 150

Lord Buddha, 40
- Statue (7.5 Meter Tall), 40

Loss of Identity, 130

Magspons, 27

Maharaja of Jammu and Kashmir, 53

Maitreya, 34

Masjid-Sharif Chushot, 37

Major Religions, 64

Ma-lo-so, 27
Manali, 22
Manali – Leh National Highway, 147
Manmohan Singh; Finance Minister, 105
Marginalization among Ladakhis, 206
Marginalized, 136
Markets, 150, 157
Mar-po (Ladakh), 27
Marriage Ceremony, 31
Mar-Yul, 26
Mask Dances, 41
Material Culture of Consumerism, 184
Medical
  Centres, 144
  Institutions, 98, 99
Metalled Roads, 96, 148
Micro-Hydel Projects at, 60
  Basgo, 60
  Hunder, 60
  Summer, 60
Migration, 36
  Of Labour, 89
Militancy, 10, 174
  Impact of—In the Valley, 15
  In Kashmir, 10
Militant Violence, 93
Minerals, 9
Mining and Quarrying, 76
Ministry of Defence, 147
Minority (ies), 50, 51
Mirza Haidar Dughlat, 36
Missionaries and Sages, 35
Modern Equipment and Technology, 90
Modernization, 63, 111, 203, 205
  And Globalization, 135, 138
  Forces, 211, 213, 218
Mohra Hydro-Electric Plant, 82
Monasteries, 29, 30, 41
  Chemreay, 41
  Matho, 41
  Phiyang, 40, 41
  Spituk, 41
  Thiksey, 41
Monastery on Hill Rock at Shargole, 45
Monastic Festivals, 41
Mongols of Tibet (Tibetan) Origin, 28, 35
Monks to Tibet for Higher Learning, 35
Mons, 27, 30
  Buddhism, 33, 34
Motilal Nehru Committee, 50
Mountain Passes in Ladakh, 25-26
Movement for Autonomy, 47
MUF, 58
Mulbek, 34, 36
Multi-Dimensional Development, 147
Multi-Nationals, 135
Multiple Nationalities, 49
Murals, 34
Muslim
  Action Committee (MAC), 57
  Countries, 10, 63
  Festivals, 37
  Majority Kashmir, 13
  Majority of Kargil, 14
  Monuments in Ladakh, (MM), 37
  Of Leh, 177
  Population, 65
Muslims Of Kargil, 65, 177
Muzzafarabad District, 11

Nagin Club, 107
Namgyal, P, LBA Leader, 60
Nation Building, 205
National Conference, 57, 61, 210
  Conference Leaders, 61
Nationalism, 63, 203, 204
Nationalist Forces, 63
Natural Disasters, 211
Nawroz, 38
New Hydel Policy, 88
NHPC, 82-84
Nigeria, 49
Nimo Bazgo HEP, 87
Nomadic Groups, 26
  Do'ng, 26
  Meyak, 26
  Sme, 26
Nomads, 26, 34
North
  East, 11, 52
    Frontier Agency, (NEFA) Type Administration, 59, 209
  Eastern States of India, 51, 204
  West India, 22

West Ladakh, 37
Northern
Frontier Dependencies, 11
Ireland, 120
Tibet, 27
Nubra Valley, 24
Nubra—Bogdang, 38
Nun-Kun Peaks, 24
Nunneries, 30
Nyathistani Princes, 36

Old Customs and Traditions, 139
Ouster of Foreigners in US and UK, 136, 212

Padama Sambhav, Buddhist Scholar and Monk, 33, 41
Pakistan, 11, 63, 120
Aggression, 53
And China, 88
And Jammu, 148
Forces, 53
Occupied Kashmir, (POK), 22, 23, 40
Pangong lake, 23
Partition, 10, 50
Tract of Events of-, 10
Passes
Baralacha, 22
Fotu La, 22
Rohtang, 22
Tang Lang La, 22
Warwan, 44
Zoji La, 22
PDP, 210
People of
Jammu and Kashmir, 120, 122
Jammu and Ladakh, 58
Kargil and Leh, 167, 169, 170
Ladakh (POL), 16, 17, 120, 122, 124, 133, 146, 163, 176, 177, 186, 195
Peoples Republic of China, 200
Phiyang Monastery, 40, 41
Physiography of Kashmir, 11
Plant Protection Measures, 90
Pluralism, 204
Political
Autonomy, 16
Democratization in Jammu and Kashmir, 15
Development After Partition, 53
Factors, 160
Grievances, 160
Mobilization of People, 47
Status, 188
System, 50
Politics of
Integration, 56
Isolation, 56
Privilege, 56
Polyandry, 28
tradition among Ladakhis, 28
Poonch
Jagir in Jammu and Kashmir, 11
Rajauri and Akhnoor, Muslim Dominated Towns, 57
Population of Leh and Kargil Districts, 209
Postal and Communication Services, 149
Post-Offices in Jammu and Kashmir, 97
Post-Tibetan Period, 34
Pothoari Speaking Western Tract, 11
Poverty and Unemployment, 75, 80
Power
Decentralization, 186
Development in Jammu and Kashmir, 82
Generation, 82, 85, 87
Statistics, 85
Projects in the State (PPS), 83
Bemina, 83
Chenani, 83
Ganderbal, 83
Gat Turbine, 83
Leh, 83
Lower Jhelum, 83
Mohra, 83
Others, 83
Upper Singh, 83
Sector, 84, 215
Structure, 15
Praja Parishad Agitation in Jammu, 58
Pre-Tibetan Buddhist Rock Engraving, 34
Primary Health Centres, 99, 143
Princely States of India, 11

Principle Languages of State, 67
Problem of Kashmir, 10
Protectionism, 135
Public Service Commission Board, 80
Punjab, 165, 204
Purukiri and Zanskari, 32

Quebec Province in Canada, 120

Races, 26
  Aryans, 26
  Baltis, 26
  Dards, 26
  Mongolia, 26
  Mons, 26
Raghunath Temple Jammu, 108
Red Cap Sect of Buddhists, 41
Referendum, 49
Region of Jammu, 13
  And Ladakh, 95, 186, 213
  And Ladakh and Kashmir, 55, 76, 138, 205
  Kargil, 186
  Kashmir, 13, 14, 75, 76, 207, 217
  Ladakh, 14, 38, 111, 112, 136, 140, 154, 167, 184, 191, 215
  Ladakh and Jammu, 72, 105, 111, 120, 210, 217
Regional
  And Cultural Identity, 9
  Autonomy, 186
  Hill Council, 201
Regionalism, 58
Religious
  Practices, 62
  Settlements, 34
Resettlement Bill, 61
Rgyalbum Ldey, 36
Rgyal-Rigs (Royals), 29
Riasi, 58
Right of Self-Determination, 47
Rinchen Shah, Son of King Morup Gon of Ladakh, 35
River
  Indus, 19, 23, 25, 40, 87
  Nubra, 25
  Penze, 24
  Shyok, 19, 24, 25
  Shyok, Zanskar, 40
  Sindhu and Suru, 153
  Suru, 24, 25, 87
  Terraces, 24
  Zanskar, 19, 25
Roads, 96, 111, 147, 208
  And Transport, 156
Rock Carvings around Kha-La-Che, 27
Role of
  ISI, 10
  Jammu and Kashmir Armed Police, 60
  Language, race, religion and culture, 120
RSS, 61

Sadarud-din-Rinchen Shah, 35
Saint Bulbul Shah, 35
Saka Tribe of Central Asia, 44
Salal Stage-I, II, NAPC Projects, 83
Samba, 58
Sawalkot project, 83
Scheduled Commercial Banks, 102
Secessional Movements, 160
Secularism, 159
Segregation of Region, 176
Self-Determination, 203
Sengge Namgyal, ruler of Ladakh, 40
Sense of alienation Among Ladakhis, 174
Separate
  Constitution (J&K), 178
    Citizenship, 178
    Flag (J&K), 178
  Culture Identity, 199
  Political Status, 204
Sericulture, 103
Serkha Gompa, 28
Shafat Nallah, 24
Shah Miri Dynasty, 36
Shawl, Pashmina, Tweed, Wood and Brassware, 39
Shey Palace (Seat of Pre-Tibetan Kings), 40
Shay Yokma, 37
Sheikh Abdullah, 59
  Government, 43
Shia
  And Sunnis, 37

Dominated Kargil, 59
Muslims, 37, 59
Shikaras, 106
Shiv Sena, 57, 61
Sikhs, 81
Silk Route, 21, 38
Sinkiang Province of China, 11, 18
Skardu (Ladakh), 11
Of Pakistan Occupied Kashmir, 22
Skitde Nemagon, 35
Sku-Drag (Nobles), 29
Skyid-Ide-Nyimagon, 28
Small Industries, 103, 105
Handicrafts, 104
Raw Silk, 104
Sericulture, 104
Tourism, 104
Woollen, 104
Small Scale Industries, 102, 105
Social
And Cultural Life of Ladakh, 124
And Cultural Traditions, 169
And Economic Factors, 159
Factors, 119
Race, language, religion, Culture, etc., 119
Structure, 119, 130, 184
Societal Disparities, 159
Society of Ladakh, 207
Socio-Economic
Societal Disparities, 159
Society of Ladakh, 207
Socio-Economic
And Political Development, 16
Benefits, 106
Classification, 29
Development, 51
Forces, 119
South Africa, 49, 120
Southern Russia, 22
Soviet Union's Aggression of Afghanistan, 62
Spain, 49
Special Status, 53
To State of Jammu and Kashmir, 178
Under Article-370, 180
Srinagar Bar Association, 57
Srinagar-Kargil-Leh National Highway, 147
Srinagar-Leh National Highway, 19
ST (Scheduled Tribe) Status, 61, 163, 176, 207, 209
State
Formations, 203
Legislative Assembly, 193, 195, 210
State of Jammu and Kashmir, 9-11, 15-17, 38, 52-55, 62, 64, 75, 81, 88, 89, 94, 99, 100, 108-110, 120, 165, 186, 198, 204-207, 214
Population, 12
System, 204
State's Legislative Bodies, 60
Statehood, 14
Or Union Territory Status, 9
Status of
Ladakh Vis-à-vis Jammu and Kashmir, 17,
Scheduled Tribe (ST), 17, 61, 163, 176, 207, 209
Statue of Lord Chamba, 45
Storma-Phang-Ches Ritual, 32
Sub-Region of Ladakh, 188
Sub-Regions of Leh and Kargil, 167
Sultan
Sayed of Kashgar, 36
Shihab-ud-din, 36
Sikander Khan, 36
Sunnah Sect, 65
Suru
Kartsey, 36
River Basin, 19
Valley, 24, 25
Switzerland, 49

Tak Thok, 41
Tarchoks, 31
Tashi Tsegspal, 35
Teachers, Doctors, etc., 158
Technology, 135, 211
Telecommunication, 208
And Health, 98
Temples and Monasteries, 34, 40, 41
Territory of Kashmir, 11
Terrorism, 10, 171
Thikse Monstery, 40
Famous for Architectural Beauty, 40

Tibet, 11, 21, 33, 216
  And Afghanistan, 11
  Yarkand, Kashmir and Turkistan, 38
Tibetan (s), 35, 67
  Buddhism, 34
  Language, 28
Timber, 106
Tourism, 80, 93, 104, 106, 108, 111, 112, 133, 140, 208
  In Kashmir, 107
  Industry, 39, 108
Tourist Places, popular, 39
  Chanlang, 39
  Choglumsar, 39
  Drass, 39
  Kargil, 39
  Leh, 39
  Nubra, 39
  Padum, 39
  Suru Valley, Shyok Valley, Sankoo, Rangdung etc., 39, 107
  Thicksey, 39
  Zangla, 39
  Zanskar, 39
Tourist Spots, 107
  Ahrabal Phase-I, 107
  Batote, 107
  Bungus, 107
  Duksum Phase I, 107
  Mantalai, 107
  Salal Lake, 107
  Sonamarg, 107
  Wullar Lake, 107
  Yusmarg, 107
Towns of Leh and Kargil, 157
Tractorisation, 90
Traditional Values, 128
Transnational Groups, 135, 212
Transport, 140
  System, 102
Trekkers, 24
Tribal Status of Ladakhis, 16, 160
Trifurcation of Jammu and Kashmir, 214, 219
Tsang And Purang Provinces, 35
Tunnelling, 216
Turkmenistan, 11
Turuk Mosque, 37
Tyakshi Mosque, 37

UK, 49
Umsai La, 45
Unitary Constitution, 55, 62
University of Kashmir, 71
US, 48
UT Status, 59, 60, 65, 167, 177, 181, 201, 209
Uttarakhand, 165

Vague Ideologies, 50
Vaishno Devi Shrine, 108
Valleys of-, 24
  Drass, 24
  Indus, 24
  Kashmir, 22
  Nubra, 24
  Shyok, 24
  Zanskar, 24
Voting Right, 191

Wakha Mulbek, 45
Wall Paintings of Lord Buddha, 40
Warwan Pass, 44
Wazir
  Commission (Committee), 56, 58
  JN, Chief Justice, 58
Weaving, 157
Western
  China, 22
  Tibet, 28, 34
White Collar Jobs, 82
Working Force, 77-79

Yarlung Dynasty of Tibet, 32
Yorkshire, 49
Yum-e-Hussaini, festival 38

Zain-ul-Abidin's Invasion of Ladakh, 36
Zanskar, 19, 24, 27, 45
  And Suru Valley, 44
  Block of Kargil District, 33
  Valley, 25
Za-Zung, 27
Zoji La Pass, 22
Zorawar Singh, General, 44